# Food for Drinks Parties

# FOOD FOR DRINKS PARTIES

by
Alison Wilkinson

**FABER AND FABER LIMITED**
3 Queen Square London

*First published in 1977*
*by Faber and Faber Limited*
*3 Queen Square London WC1*
*Printed in Great Britain by*
*Redwood Burn Ltd. Trowbridge and Esher*
*All rights reserved*

*© Alison Wilkinson, 1977*

**British Library Cataloguing in Publication Data**

Wilkinson Alison
    Food for drinks parties.
    1. Entertaining 2. Cookery
    I. Title
    641.5'62               TX731

    ISBN 0-571-11056-8
    ISBN 0-571-11177-7 Pbk

TO MY HUSBAND ERIC
who uncomplainingly sampled and
constructively criticized
most of the recipes in this book

# CONTENTS

# INTRODUCTION

## 1. Quantities

The recipes in this book are designed for a drinks party for 18–20 guests. Because of this, most of the recipes produce 36 items, so that one can hand each dish round twice. Some people will always refuse, and this allows for the others to have two, and an occasional person, three.

Plan to provide something to eat approximately every fifteen minutes. For up to nine guests, halve the recipes, and, for more than twenty increase the ingredients in proportion.

### Sauces and Dips

It is difficult to say how much sauce, or how much dip, one should allow. Some people will take only a little, others will scoop up all they possibly can. I have allowed 2 dl (⅓ pint) of sauce, and 170 g (6 oz) cold dip for 36 items. It's better to be overgenerous than have people scraping the bottom of the bowl.

### Cheese

Cheese can vary enormously in strength, and, for that reason, in some of the recipes, I have left the amount slightly open.

### Seasoning

It is also difficult to be dogmatic over quantities of salt, pepper, spices and herbs. This is not only a matter of taste, but spices and herbs vary a great deal, particularly with age. Where quantities have been given there is usually a good reason, though they should only be treated as a guide, and where no specific amount is mentioned, the quantity required generally depends on the other ingredients present. Olives may have been stored in oil or brine, anchovies in oil or salt, and so on.

### Eggs

Any size of egg is suitable, unless specified otherwise.

**Variations**

It is not possible within the scope of this book to give all the variations that can be tried with the basic recipes. But with a little practice and imagination you can vary the different ingredients to your own taste, or substitute something you have available for one of my ingredients. For example, cold chicken, ham, salami, tuna, peeled shrimps or prawns can often be substituted for each other. Recipes with cream cheese might be varied by adding a little finely chopped onion, olives, sweet peppers, anchovies, chives or pineapple, or minced chicken or celery, or sweet chutney. Other recipes can be adapted by incorporating a garnish such as nuts, chopped sweet peppers, etc., into a cream cheese or mayonnaise mixture and adding another garnish. Methods or ingredients for one recipe may give you an idea for adapting another. There are endless ways of making a recipe more or less elaborate, or more or less strongly flavoured, to suit your taste, your budget, or what you happen to have available or is in season at the time.

# 2. Measurements

Quantities have been given both in metric and imperial measurements. As 1 oz = 28.35 g the metric measurements have been rounded off to the nearest convenient figure (see the table below). In the course of cooking a recipe, please use one set of measurements or the other, and never some of each.

| | |
|---|---|
| 300 ml or 3 dl | = ½ pint |
| 450 ml or 4½ dl | = ¾ pint |
| 600 ml or 6 dl | = 1 pint |
| 1 dl | = 5 tablespoons |
| half a litre | = just under a pint |

| | |
|---|---|
| 1 rounded tablespoon flour | = 30 g (1 oz) |
| 1 rounded and 1 level tablespoon cornflour | = 30 g (1 oz) |
| 1 level tablespoon sugar | = 30 g (1 oz) |
| 2 liquid tablespoons butter | = 30 g (1 oz) |
| 7 level tablespoons fresh breadcrumbs | = 30 g (1 oz) |
| 3½ level tablespoons finely grated cheese | = 30 g (1 oz) |
| 5 rounded teaspoons curry powder or spices | = 30 g (1 oz) |
| 1 rounded and 1 level tablespoon gelatin | = 30 g (1 oz) |
| 1 rounded tablespoon aspic jelly crystals | = 30 g (1 oz) |
| 1 rounded and 1 level tablespoon parmesan cheese | = 30 g (1 oz) |

'Spoonfuls' are always intended to be 'as much above as below'. When a level spoonful is intended, it is specifically mentioned. A 'well-rounded spoonful' means that the spoon should be filled more than a 'rounded' spoonful, though not actually heaped.

# 3. Oven Temperatures

Check that your oven temperature corresponds exactly with the temperature registering on your thermostat. It is surprising how many ovens have been set wrongly, and this can cause mistakes in baking.

The oven temperature required for most of the recipes is 200°C (400°F). This is in order to allow the baking of different savouries at the same time, or their re-heating, without constantly altering the temperature.

# 4. Butter or Margarine

In most recipes both are suitable, but on the occasions when I have mentioned only butter it is because I feel that on those occasions it is better for the flavour. But if for medical reasons butter should be avoided, margarine can always be substituted.

# 5. Egg and Breadcrumb Dressing

Savoury balls which are to be deep fried should be rolled in flour, dipped into a mixture of egg and water, and covered in fresh white breadcrumbs.

The easiest way to do this is to roll all the mixture into balls first, using the palms of the hands, dropping them, as they are rolled, into a bowl of flour. When they have all been shaped, roll them around in the flour, to make sure they are all well covered. Drop them one at a time into a bowl of beaten egg and water, lifting each one out immediately, and dropping it into a bowl of breadcrumbs. After dropping five or six, roll the bowl of breadcrumbs around in such a way that the balls become coated. Take each one out, and roll it again in your palms, pressing the crumbs in firmly. Repeat with the rest of the balls. In this way you avoid a build-up of flour, egg and breadcrumbs on your own hands instead of on the balls.

### Egg and Breadcrumb Dressing – white sauce base

When making balls from a thick white sauce, avoid trying to shape the balls without first coating them with flour. First, chill the mixture well. Then take up a little in a teaspoon, and push the mixture off the teaspoon into the flour with a finger. Tip the flour over, after which it can safely be picked up and rolled. It doesn't matter if they are not completely spherical. The frying process will turn the strangest shapes into perfect spheres.

### Egg and Breadcrumb Dressing – over a breadcrumbs base

When making balls containing a high proportion of breadcrumbs, you may have to squeeze the ingredients together in the palm of your hand to make them adhere, before rolling in the flour and egg and breadcrumb dressing. This may appear very unstable, but the coating will hold it together. These balls swell considerably when fried, so start small.

### Shallow Frying of Meat Balls, etc.

Never deep fry meatballs that have been rolled in flour alone. They will shrink too much. Use shallow fat, and always drain on absorbent paper.

# 6. Deep Frying

This should always take place at about 200° C (400° F), that is, when the very first sign of bluish smoke rises from the hot fat. If the fat is too hot the outside will be cooked before the middle, and the kitchen will fill with smoke. If the fat is too cool, the result will not only be greasy, but in the case of meatballs, for example, the items may actually disintegrate in the fat. If in doubt buy a fat thermometer. Always drain on absorbent paper.

# 7. Pastry Brush

This is used a great deal either to dampen pastry in order to make different surfaces stick together, or to paint milk or egg and water on the top to help to brown it. It is far easier, in my opinion, to use a 2½ cm (1 in) house painting brush, and far cheaper, but buy one of a good quality or the bristles may come out.

# 8. Deep Freezing

Small savouries can be damaged if packed directly into containers. They should instead be frozen quickly on an open tray in the freezer, and, as soon as firm, transferred to the containers, sealed and labelled. They should be removed for re-heating while still frozen, placed on baking trays, and allowed to thaw fully before re-heating.

### Deep Freezing of Meatballs, etc.

(a) The uncooked mixture can be frozen in one lump. It can then be thawed and rolled into small balls, dressed and fried. Allow plenty of time, up to two or three hours, for thawing; or

(b) The uncooked mixture can be shaped into balls, rolled in flour, or flour, egg and breadcrumb, and frozen. In that case the balls must first be frozen on an open tray, and, when firm, packed into containers, or they will stick together. They should be separated again before thawing. Only 30 minutes need be allowed for thawing, before frying; or

(c) The fried balls may, with care, be packed directly into containers when cold, and frozen. They must be separated again before thawing, allowing 30 minutes, and re-heated in the oven at 200° C (400° F), for approximately 6 minutes.

# 9. Acknowledgements

The author wishes to thank the many authors whose cookery books have formed the background for many of her experiments. These include:

*The Great Scandinavian Cookbook*, edited by J. Audrey Allison; *The Robert Carrier Cookbook*, by Robert Carrier; *The Constance Spry Cookery Book*, by Constance Spry and Rosemary Hume; *Mastering the Art of French Cooking*, by Simone Beck, Louisette Bertholle and Julia Child; *Soups and Hors d'œuvres*, by Marika Hanbury-Tenison; *Deep-Freeze Cookery*, by Marika Hanbury-Tenison; *French Provincial Cooking*, by Elizabeth David; *A Book of Mediterranean Food*, by Elizabeth David; *Italian Food*, by Elizabeth David; *Middle Eastern Cookery*, by Claudia Roden

# 1
# THE DRINKS PARTY

The food at a drinks party should look nice and taste nice, and supplement the activities of drinking and talking. Handing it round provides an easy way for the hostess to move among her guests, and gives her an excuse to leave one group and move on to another.

It is also, as everyone knows, a bad thing to drink on an empty stomach. At a party at which a lot of drink will be consumed, start off with some fairly solid food, such as stuffed hard-boiled eggs, sausage rolls or baby pizzas.

## Variety

Think all the time, when planning the food, of providing contrasts in colour, flavour and texture. A selection of cold canapés looks very attractive. But if this is followed by more canapés, and yet more canapés, it becomes monotonous. Offer instead something hot followed by something cold, something rich with something light, and something highly-seasoned with something mild.

A rough guide is to provide something to eat approximately every fifteen minutes. You will probably have in the room a few bowls of nuts, olives, etc., for those who want to eat in between.

If you are leaving plates of cold food around, hoping that the guests will help themselves, put them on a central table, if the room is not too crowded, or under a bright lamp. On side tables, in the dark corners of the room, they go unnoticed and uneaten. And as soon as the plates are nearly empty, remove them. There is nothing sadder than a solitary canapé.

## Sizes and Shapes

Everything should be very small, and the 'one-mouthful' size is usually the best. Nobody likes to have an avalanche of pastry crumbs down the front of his suit as he bites into a large tartlet, or to find a hidden slice of tough ham, or a whole slice of cucumber, half-bitten through, emerging unexpectedly from the middle of a sandwich.

And watch the garnishes! A spray of dill can stand so high that you wonder if you will ever get it into your mouth, and you haven't a spare hand to remove it. A sprinkling of chopped parsley looks nicer.

*The Drinks Party*
## Planning the Food

Think who your guests are before deciding what to prepare. It's a waste of time to make dozens of finicky little canapés for people with hearty appetites, or to go to a lot of trouble with *haute cuisine* recipes for unappreciative guests. And, incidentally, very few people like aspic.

And don't disguise the food. Some people cannot, and others prefer not to eat certain foods, either for health or religious reasons, or because they just don't like them. Pork and all kinds of shellfish are obvious dangers, but some people are allergic to quite ordinary things like eggs and green peppers. Don't garnish so heavily that you cannot see what's inside. Stick a flag on the plate, or say what's in it, as you hand it round.

It's kind to provide a few light things for slimmers, such as stuffed celery or grapes, open sandwiches made with salad, crudités, or, if you can get it, qvark. This is a low-calorie cottage-cheese-like spread, which comes in a wide variety of flavours. It used to be available only in Denmark and Germany, but now it's more universally obtainable.


## Cigarettes

These always used to be provided, either in open boxes, or distributed round the room in glasses, with matches in an ashtray near by. No one expects to be offered cigarettes these days, and those who smoke carry their own, and their lighters. A lot of people feel it is wrong to encourage smoking by offering cigarettes, though they don't object to people smoking their own.


## Drinks

Here there are several possibilities.

You can offer a large selection of drinks, gin, whisky, sherry, vodka, etc., plus all the soft drinks needed to go with them, and perhaps also a cocktail. In that case you will need a barman, or the help of a guest. It is far too much work for the host alone. He will have to spend the whole evening fetching and carrying glasses, when he should be talking to his guests. And it is no use asking guests to help themselves; some will, but some won't, and the ones that won't will be the ones who will complain afterwards that they got nothing to drink.

If you want to avoid employing a barman, or asking a guest to help, stick to wine, such as a sparkling white, or provide just one alternative, perhaps a Bloody Mary, or whisky. The host can then wander among his guests, bottle or decanter in hand, refilling the glasses as he goes.

Try to provide a non-alcoholic alternative for teetotallers and drivers. If you are serving Bloody Mary, offer tomato juice; if wine or other drinks, perhaps grape juice and soda, or apple juice and ice.

It is extremely difficult to state dogmatically how much drink one should allow per person. It depends on the length of the party as well as on the capacity of the guests. If serving a selection of drinks, or cocktails, one should allow a minimum of three drinks per person, and, if wine, half a bottle, for a two-hour party. But one might need a lot more.

Most wine merchants will supply wines and spirits on a sale or return basis, as long as the bottles haven't been opened, so open them only when needed.

## Glasses

Wine merchants will also, sometimes, provide glasses if you are buying wine or spirits from them, charging only for breakages. If possible, use the tulip-shaped glasses for wine, and you will have fewer spills on the carpet. The wide champagne glasses are definitely 'out'.

## Space

Remove the doors if you are short of space. The doors on most modern houses lift off easily, but it may be necessary to use a screwdriver in an older house.

## Noise

The quantity of noise is related directly to the amount of light. If the noise gets too much, dim the lights.

Despite the criticism of 'canned music' it's really quite a good idea to begin the evening with soft music in the background. There tends to be a lack of conversation as the first guests arrive, particularly if they've never met before, and music can help to make people relax. The volume of sound will soon rise to drown the music, and the tape needn't be replaced.

## Heat

People generate a lot of heat. The room must be warm to come into, but before it gets too hot, turn the heat down. Once a room is too hot it is too late. Then the only way to cool it is to open a window or an outside door, and let in the icy blast, which not only chills the guests, but can act as a damper on the party.

## Introducing People

Once more than a few guests have arrived, it becomes difficult to make any more formal introductions, except, perhaps to those standing near the door, and the host has, to some extent, to rely on the newly-arrived to find their own way round the room, and to introduce themselves.

But don't forget that a lot of noise doesn't necessarily mean that *everyone* is happy. It is easy to find oneself cornered by someone with whom one has nothing in common, with no apparent way of escape. Guests are often grateful to be moved around occasionally, or to have a new face introduced into the circle.

On the other hand, it can be very annoying to be enjoying oneself, and to be dragged across the room by an over-conscientious hostess towards someone who 'is simply longing to meet you'.

One of the most important skills in running a drinks party is to know who to move when.

# 2
# SAVOURIES

## 2(a). Assorted Cold Savouries

**EACH RECIPE MAKES 36 SAVOURIES UNLESS
OTHERWISE STATED**

*Savouries*

## Salted Almonds   Makes 225 g (8 oz)

225 g (8 oz) almonds with
 skins on or blanched and
 skinned, as preferred

1½ tablespoons corn oil
1 level teaspoon salt

To blanch and skin, place the almonds in boiling water and simmer for 1 minute. Pour off the boiling water and immediately cover with cold. The nuts will then slip out of the skins very easily. Heat the oil in a pan, add the almonds and fry very gently for 2 minutes. Sprinkle with salt while still hot.

Not suitable for freezing. May be prepared in advance and kept fresh in an airtight tin for several weeks. Can also be served hot.

## Devilled Nuts   Makes 225 g (8 oz)

225 g (8 oz) almonds, blanched
 and skinned (see previous
 recipe)
15 g (½ oz) butter

½ level teaspoon castor sugar
1 level teaspoon dry mustard
1 level teaspoon curry powder
1 level teaspoon salt

Heat the butter in a pan, add the nuts and fry very gently until lightly browned. Mix the dry ingredients in a bowl, add the nuts and toss until well coated.

Not suitable for freezing. May be prepared in advance and kept fresh in an airtight tin for several weeks. Can also be served hot.

## Fried Chick-peas   Makes 225 g (8 oz)
(Poor Man's Nuts)

225 g (8 oz) dried chick-peas
60 g (2 oz) butter

1 level teaspoon salt

Soak the chick-peas for 24 hours. Drain and simmer in gently boiling water for approximately 1 hour or longer, according to the age of the peas. Drain when just tender, and dry. Fry very gently for 1–2 minutes in melted butter and sprinkle with salt while still hot.

Not suitable for freezing. May be prepared in advance and kept fresh in an airtight tin for several weeks. Can also be served hot, or 'devilled' with a little cayenne and curry powder mixed into the salt.

## Stuffed Grapes

36 large grapes (approximately
 250 g, 9 oz)

210 g (7 oz) soft cream cheese

Slit the grapes down one side only and remove the pips. Roll the cream cheese into 36 small balls, and insert one into each grape.

Not suitable for freezing. May be prepared a few hours in advance and kept chilled.

### Stuffed Celery

*1 small head of celery (tinned is not suitable)*
*180 g (6½ oz) soft cream cheese, or mix together 110 g (4 oz) cheddar and 45 g (1½ oz) blue cheese*
*3 or more tablespoons milk or thin cream*

For the garnish:
*chopped parsley, or chopped nuts, or chopped chives, or red or black lumpfish caviare*

Mix the milk or cream into the cheese. Cut the celery stems into 36 pieces, each approximately 2½ cm (1 in) long – wide ones can be cut in half lengthwise. Pipe the cheese into the stems, and sprinkle with the garnish.

### Stuffed Sweet Peppers

*2 red sweet peppers each weighing approximately 90 g (3 oz), with seeds removed*
*90 g (3 oz) soft cream cheese*
*1 teaspoon lemon juice*
*60 g (2 oz) pineapple, finely chopped*
*20 g (¾ oz) walnuts, finely chopped*

*20 g (¾ oz) ham, or salmon, or cold chicken, or tuna, finely chopped*
*20 g (¾ oz) apple, or celery, finely chopped*
*1 teaspoon gelatine*
*2 tablespoons hot water*

Dissolve the gelatine in the hot water, and mix with the lemon juice and cream cheese. Add all other ingredients and mix well. Fill the peppers with the mixture, making sure you fill every crevice. Chill, preferably overnight, cut in thick slices and then into chunks. Serve cold, on sticks.

Not suitable for freezing. May be prepared in advance, but sliced only a short time before serving.

### Stuffed Dates

*36 dates (approximately 280 g, 10 oz)*

*210 g (7 oz) soft cream cheese*

Slit the dates down one side only, and remove the stones. Roll the cream cheese into small marble-sized balls, and stuff into the dates. Serve on cocktail sticks.

Not suitable for freezing. May be prepared a few hours in advance and kept cool.

### Anchovy Olives

*36 stuffed olives, approximately 110 g (4 oz)*

*18 tinned anchovies, approximately 90 g (3 oz)*

Cut each anchovy lengthwise, starting one third of the way down one side, and ending two thirds of the way down the other. Wrap each half round one stuffed olive, and secure with a cocktail stick. Olives stuffed with almonds are particularly good.

### Salami Cones

*120 g (4 oz) salami, approximately 4 cm (1½ in) wide*
*30 g (1 oz) Mayonnaise (page 69) or tableready horseradish cream*

*30 g (1 oz) soft cream cheese*
*36 buttered bread canapés*

Remove the skin from the salami by making a slit right down one side, with a very sharp knife. Cut rings at intervals round the salami, and peel off the skin from where the incisions intersect. Cut into 36 very thin slices. Cut each slice, with scissors, from the edge to the centre. Overlap the cut edges, and press together to form a cone shape. Place on a bread base. Mix the horseradish or mayonnaise with the soft cream cheese, adding a very little milk if required, and pipe a small amount into the centre of each cone. Hold in place with a cocktail stick.

Not suitable for freezing. May be prepared a few hours in advance, and kept cool.

### Cucumber and Caviare

*18 in (46 cm) cucumber*
*120 g (4 oz) soft cream cheese*
*3 tablespoons sour or fresh cream*

*45 g (1½ oz) red or black lumpfish caviare, or peeled prawns, or shrimps, or a piece of crab or lobster*
*1 level teaspoon salt*
*2 tablespoons wine vinegar*

Cut the cucumber into 36 slices, leaving on the skin. With a sharp knife cut round just inside the skin, removing the top layer of the middle of the slice and leaving a narrow wall round the edge. Dissolve the salt and vinegar in ½ litre (1 pint) water, and soak the cucumber slices in the solution for 1 hour. Drain, and dry well. Mix the cheese with either sour or fresh cream, and fill the slices of cucumber, allowing about a teaspoon for each. Place on top the caviare, or the chosen shellfish.

## Artichoke Hearts and Caviare

This recipe comes from Fru Britta Rylander of Stockholm, Sweden.

*36 tinned artichoke hearts, as*      *75 g (3½ oz) black lumpfish*
*small as possible*                              *caviare*
                                                              *2 teaspoons lemon juice*

Drain the artichoke hearts well, and make sure the bases are flat so that they will stand steadily. Spoon the caviare into the centre of each, and sprinkle over the lemon juice.

Not suitable for freezing. May be prepared a few hours in advance and kept cool.

## Hamburger Geraucht Aalspiesse
### (Smoked Eel Canapé from Hamburg)

This recipe comes from Frau Häsi Hugo of Kronberg/Taunus, West Germany.

*3 medium eating apples*              *110 g (4 oz) smoked eel,*
*60 g (2 oz) kalbsleberwurst*          *filleted and with skin*
*(calf liver pâté sausage)*             *removed*
*3 large tinned pineapple rings*     *2 teaspoons parsley, chopped*

Peel the apples and slice each into 4 or 5 circles, and remove the core. Cut each into 2 or 3 sections, depending on the size, to form bases for the canapés. Spread each with a little of the pâté. Place a piece of smoked eel on each, and a small piece of pineapple on top. Secure with a cocktail stick to serve, and sprinkle with chopped parsley.

Not suitable for freezing, but may be prepared earlier in the day, and refrigerated.

## Cheese Marbles

For the basic recipe:
*225 g (8 oz) soft cream cheese,
or a mixture of cream
cheese and grated cheddar
or blue cheese*

For covering:
*ground almonds or hazelnuts,
or crushed cornflakes, or
fresh white or brown
breadcrumbs, or finely
chopped toasted almonds, or
chopped parsley, or grated
parmesan cheese, or
paprika, or curry powder*

Take approximately 7 g (¼ oz) of the cheese and shape into a small ball. Roll in the selected covering. Serve chilled.

Not suitable for freezing. May be prepared a few hours in advance and kept cool.

## Cheese Log

This recipe comes from Mrs Liane Mills of Montreal, Canada.

*60 g (2 oz) blue cheese
110 g (4 oz) cheddar
45 g (1½ oz) cream cheese
⅛ level teaspoon dry mustard
⅛ level teaspoon onion or
garlic powder*

*⅛ teaspoon Worcestershire
sauce
45 g (1½ oz) walnuts, or
pistachios or peanuts, finely
chopped*

Blend all ingredients together, except the nuts. Roll into a log shape, and roll in the chopped nuts. Wrap in waxed paper or foil and refrigerate until ready to serve. Place on a tray with a knife and savoury biscuits, and leave guests to help themselves.

Not suitable for freezing. May be prepared in advance and kept chilled.

## Stuffed Hard-boiled Eggs

*18 small eggs, hard-boiled
and shelled*
Garnish:
*prawns or shrimps, black or
red caviare, thin slice of*

*asparagus, chopped parsley,
pinch of paprika or curry
powder, etc.*

Filling: *see below*

Use only very fresh eggs. The yolks of eggs that have been standing for some time fall to the bottom of the egg, and the wall of white left underneath is usually too thin to hold the filling.

It is a good idea to boil one or two extra eggs, in case any break during the hard-boiling process.

Cut the eggs in half lengthwise, cut a little from the base of each, to enable it to stand more firmly, remove the yolk and fill with the selected filling, preferably by piping, or with a teaspoon. Clean the white of any spilled filling with the blade of a knife, and garnish.

SUGGESTED FILLINGS
A. Mash the yolks with 5–6 tablespoons of Mayonnaise (page 69), salt and pepper; or with 3 tablespoons mayonnaise, 3 table-spoons tomato ketchup, 1½ tablespoons curry powder, and 3 tablespoons apple chutney.
B. Fill the empty eggs with Tunafish Pâté (page 95) or Taramasalata (page 95) allowing approximately 10 g (⅓ oz) per egg, and grate the yolks over the filling. Reserve any extra yolks for egg mayon-naise.
C. Fill the empty whites with Swedish Liver Pâté (page 29) or Chic-ken Liver Pâté (page 93), allowing approximately 15 g (½ oz) per egg, and adding a little cream if necessary. Garnish with yolks as in B.
D. Mash the yolks with flaked cooked salmon, allowing approxi-mately 5 g (⅙ oz) salmon per egg, and add 5 tablespoons mayon-naise. Or substitute tunafish, or 18 anchovies, or 1 tin sardines.
E. Fry 60 g (3 oz) bacon and 180 g (6½ oz) skinned and de-pipped tomato in 3 tablespoons oil, and mix with the mashed yolks.

Not suitable for freezing. May be prepared a few hours in advance and kept cool.


## Cold Kebabs

*1 large eating apple*            *36 small prawns*
*3 medium sticks of celery*       *(approximately 140 g, 5 oz,*
                                  *after shelling)*

Quarter the apple and remove core, and remove or leave the peel as you wish. Cut the apple and celery into 36 small pieces each, using only the tender part of the celery, and thread the prawns, apple and celery onto cocktail sticks. Serve with 170 g (6 oz) Mayonnaise (page 69), Paprika Mayonnaise (page 70) or Seafood Dip (page 72).

OTHER SUGGESTIONS FOR COLD KEBABS
The following ingredients can all be used, mixed together in a variety of ways, putting 3 or 4 cubes on each stick, according to size. The quantities given are for 36 cubes of a suitable size: cheddar cheese

110 g (4 oz), pineapple (3 average-sized rings), tomatoes (4–5 small and very firm), mushrooms (very small, with stalks cut level) 120 g (4½ oz), ham 110 g (4 oz), ham rolled round cream cheese, stuffed olives, pieces of gherkin, cocktail onions, mandarin oranges, pieces of cucumber, cooked beetroot, fennel, red or green pepper, avocado pear, banana, cold chicken, crisp cos lettuce or endive, green or black grapes, radishes, mussels, cold cooked sausage, baby cocktail sausages, rolled beef, beef rolled round horseradish cream.

Not suitable for freezing. May be prepared a few hours in advance and kept cool.

## Marinated Aubergines

*2 medium-sized aubergines*
*1 teaspoon salt*
*6 tablespoons oil or olive oil*
*1 clove garlic, crushed*

For the marinade:
*Sauce Vinaigrette (page 71)*

Cut the aubergines each into 18 cubes, leaving the skins on, sprinkle with the salt, and leave in a colander for at least 2 hours to drain. Drain off any excess juice, and pat dry with absorbent paper. Fry gently in the oil, with the garlic, and marinate in a lightly seasoned vinaigrette sauce. Drain well and serve on cocktail sticks.

## Kalbsrollchen
### (Little German Veal Rolls)

This recipe comes from Frau Häsi Hugo of Kronberg/Taunus, West Germany.

*9 round slices of very thinly*
*sliced cooked veal, or ham,*
*or beef, approximately 12 cm*
*(5 in) in diameter*
*1 teaspoon parsley, chopped*
*25 walnut halves, finely*
*chopped*
*140 g (5 oz) sultanas*

*5 prunes, soaked and*
*chopped*
*1 tablespoon port or sweet*
*sherry*
*9 small cornichons or*
*gherkins*
*150 g (5½ oz) kalbsleberwurst*
*(calf liver pâté sausage)*

Mash the pâté with the port or sherry and add all the other ingredients except the cornichons and the slices of veal. Slice the cornichons lengthwise into 4. Cut the veal (or ham or beef) in half, and then in half again, to form 4 quadrants. Lay one piece of cornichon and a little of the pâté mixture along each piece and roll over into the form of a cone. Secure with a cocktail stick.

Not suitable for freezing, but may be prepared the day before and refrigerated.

### Swedish Liver Pâté     Makes 450 g (1 lb) or 50 cubes

*225 g (8 oz) calves liver (not pork or ox)*
*60 g (2 oz) pork fat, or fat bacon*
*45 g (1½ oz) onion, finely chopped*
*1 small egg, lightly beaten*
*3 tablespoons thin cream*
*45 g (1½ oz) plain flour*
*1½ tablespoons dry vermouth*

*60 g (2 oz) mushrooms (optional)*
*1 slightly rounded teaspoon salt*
*black pepper*
*3 dl (½ pint) aspic jelly solution*
*30 g (1 oz) butter or margarine for the mushrooms*
*15 g (½ oz) butter or margarine for the terrine*

If using the mushrooms, slice or chop roughly, and sauté in the butter or margarine. Mince the liver and pork fat together very finely. Add all ingredients, except the mushrooms, and blend, preferably in an electric blender till very smooth. Mix in the mushrooms by hand, and pour into the buttered terrine. Cover with foil, and then with the lid of the terrine, and place in a bainmarie (see recipe for Pork and Game Pâté, page 92). Bake at 160°C (325°F) for 1 hour 15 minutes. Top up the water if necessary. Allow to cool. When cool, pour over the aspic jelly solution, made according to the maker's instructions. This is not essential, but it helps to keep the pâté moist. Cut into 50 cubes, and serve on sticks, either alone, or with slices of pickled cucumber, gherkins, cocktail onions, etc.

Not suitable for freezing. May be prepared in advance and kept in a refrigerator for up to one week.

### Stuffed Sausages

This recipe comes from Mrs Sue Walker of Frankfurt-am-Main, West Germany.

*36 cocktail sausages, cooked and cold*
*60 g (2 oz) mixed cheeses, cheddar, parmesan, gorgonzola and edam, finely grated*
*30 g (1 oz) butter*

*1 tablespoon cream, whipped*
*pinches of dry mustard, salt and black pepper*
*2 tablespoons piquant sauce (tomato chutney, etc.)*
*2 tablespoons finely chopped almonds*

Make a slit along the length of the sausages, but do not cut right through. Open the slit and pipe with a cream cheese filling. To make the filling, beat together the cheeses, butter, dry mustard, salt and black pepper, and, when smooth, mix with the whipped cream. Dip the sausages carefully into the piquant sauce and then into the finely chopped almonds.

## Moules Biscuits

This recipe comes from Mrs Sue Walker of Frankfurt-am-Main, West Germany.

*36 savoury biscuits*               *60 g (2 oz) cheese spread*
*36 pickled mussels*                *paprika*
  *(approximately 225 g, 8 oz)*

Drain the mussels well. Spread the biscuits with the cheese, and place a mussel on top of each. Sprinkle the top liberally with paprika.

## Mushrooms Vinaigrette

*36 fresh button mushrooms*         *90 g (3 oz) soft cream cheese*
  *(approximately 225 g, 8 oz)*     *2 tablespoons thin cream*
*3 tablespoons oil*                 *Sauce Vinaigrette (page 71)*

Remove the stalks of the mushrooms carefully, to leave a hollow in each mushroom, and fry gently in the oil. Marinate in the vinaigrette, preferably overnight. Drain well. Mash the cream cheese with 2 tablespoons thin cream, and fill each hollow with the mixture. Sprinkle with chopped parsley or chives. Can be served plain without the filling.

Not suitable for freezing. May be prepared a few hours in advance and kept cool.

## Fried Bacon Rinds

*bacon rinds*

Fry the rinds very slowly indeed, in their own fat, until they become crisp. When cool, break into 2½ cm (1 in) lengths. Make quite certain they have cooked long enough, or they will be tough and chewy.

## Tapinade            Makes 180 g (6 oz)

*60 g (2 oz) black olives, before
   stoning
60 g (2 oz) green olives, before
   stoning
1 level tablespoon capers
1 yolk of a hard-boiled egg*

*5 large anchovy fillets in oil
pinch of fresh thyme if
   available
2 or more tablespoons olive
   oil*

Pound all the ingredients together, or pulverize in a blender, till they
have amalgamated, and formed a thick spread. If too thick, or too
strong, add more olive oil. If too salty, add more oil and egg yolk. To
avoid saltiness, use olives which have been stored in oil and not in
brine. Serve on fingers of hot toast.

Suitable for freezing, or for preparing in advance and storing for
several weeks in a refrigerator.

### Stuffed Cabbage Leaves

This recipe is from Frau Häsi Hugo of Kronberg/Taunus, West Germany.

*10 small cabbage leaves (red
   or white)
130 g (4½ oz) tunafish in oil
75 g (2½ oz) onion, finely
   chopped*

*2 tablespoons oil
45 g (1½ oz) fresh white
   breadcrumbs
2 eggs lightly beaten
pinch salt and black pepper*

Simmer the cabbage leaves for 5 minutes in boiling salted water.
Remove from the water and leave to drain. Make the stuffing. Sauté
the chopped onion in the oil for 5–10 minutes or till soft. Add the
tunafish, breadcrumbs, eggs and seasonings. Mix together, or blend
in an electric blender, if preferred. Divide the mixture between the
leaves, rolling them into little rolls as in Dolmades (page 37). Lay
close together in a dish with a little stock, or the water in which the
cabbage has boiled, to come half-way up the rolls. Cover and simmer very gently for 20 minutes. Allow to cool in the stock, preferably
overnight. Remove from the dish and slice each roll into 3 or 4
pieces. Serve cold on cocktail sticks, either alone or with a suitable
dip.

SUGGESTED SAUCE
*110 g (4 oz) yoghourt
1 teaspoon icing sugar*

*1 teaspoon paprika*

Mix the ingredients together and pour over the rolls when cool.
Leave to refrigerate overnight if possible.

Not suitable for freezing, but may be prepared the day before and refrigerated, as suggested above.

### Crudités
(Raw Vegetables)

Prepare matchsticks of carrots, beetroot, young turnip or parsnip. Cut pieces of red or green sweet peppers, celery, fennel, cauliflower, raw French beans, chicory leaves.

Put on cocktail sticks radishes, very small Brussels sprouts, very firm tomatoes, mushrooms, marinated mushrooms (page 30), marinated aubergines (page 28), cocktail onions, or cubes of gherkin.

1. Those not requiring cocktail sticks can be put in piles on a tray, with one large bowl of dip in the centre, or two or three dips, contrasting both in colour and flavour.
2. Those requiring sticks can be stuck into half a red or green cabbage, cut side down, or into a large polished apple, half a pineapple, or even a large lemon, making sure each time that the base is secure.
3. Dips (pages 69–76) can be placed in bowls, or in a hollowed-out melon or pineapple. The top of the pineapple can be left on until just before serving.
4. Bowls of crisps or savoury biscuits can be available as well for using up any left-over dip.

# 2(b). Assorted Hot Savouries

**EACH RECIPE MAKES 36 SAVOURIES**

## Stuffed Dates in Bacon Rolls

*36 dates (approximately 300 g,      12 thin rashers bacon*
*10 oz)                              (approximately 170 g, 6 oz)*
*120 g (4½ oz) gruyère cheese,*
*or soft cream cheese*

1. Slit the dates and remove the stones. Cut each rasher into 3, and stretch each piece lengthwise. Stuff the dates with a small piece of gruyère, or a small piece of the cream cheese rolled into a ball, and wrap in the bacon. Either secure with a stick, or pack together so close that they cannot unroll.
2. Bake at 200°C (400°F) for 6–7 minutes. Serve hot, on cocktail sticks.

Not suitable for freezing. May be prepared in advance to the end of 1. Continue from 2.

## Stuffed Prunes in Bacon Rolls

*36 prunes (approximately           12 thin rashers of bacon*
*300 g, 10 oz)                       (approximately 170 g, 6 oz)*

*120 g (4½ oz) gruyère, cut in
  small pieces, or 170 g (6 oz)
  soft cream cheese mixed
  with 40 g (1½ oz) toasted*

*chopped almonds, or 180 g
  (6½ oz) sausagemeat, rolled
  into 36 small balls*

1. Soak the prunes for several hours or overnight, and stone if necessary, but do not cook.
2. Stuff the prunes with the selected stuffing, or leave plain. Cut each rasher into 3, and stretch each piece lengthwise. Wrap round the prunes and either secure with a stick or pack so close that they cannot unroll.
3. Bake at 200°C (400°F) for 8–9 minutes. Serve hot on sticks.

Suitable for freezing after completing 2, unless using gruyère or cream cheese. To cook, thaw for 45 minutes, and continue with 3. May be prepared in advance to the end of 2. Continue with 3.

## Stuffed Bacon Rolls

*110 g (4 oz) onion, finely
  chopped
110 g (4 oz) mushroom or
  tomato, finely chopped
60 g (2 oz) fresh breadcrumbs
3 teaspoons parsley, finely
  chopped*

*3½ tablespoons oil
1 small egg, lightly beaten
18 rashers bacon
  (approximately 225 g, 8 oz)
salt and pepper*

1. Fry the onion and mushrooms (or tomatoes) gently in the oil till soft. Add the breadcrumbs and the parsley, and continue to fry until the breadcrumbs have absorbed the fat and become crisp. Cool. Add the beaten egg, and mix well. Cut the bacon rashers in half, place 1 teaspoonful of the mixture on each, and roll tightly.
2. Lay the rolls on the baking tray with the open seam downwards. Bake at 200°C (400°F) for 8 minutes.

Suitable for freezing after completing 1. To cook, thaw for 30 minutes, and continue from 2. May be prepared in advance (a) to the end of 1. Continue with 2. Or (b) to the end of 2. Re-heat for 4–5 minutes.

## Stuffed Olives in Bacon Rolls

*36 stuffed olives,
  approximately 110 g (4 oz)*

*12 rashers very thin bacon,
  approximately 170 g (6 oz)*

1. Cut each rasher into 3, stretch slightly lengthwise, and wrap round a stuffed olive.

2. Bake at 200°C (400°F) for 6–7 minutes.

Not suitable for freezing. May be prepared in advance to the end of 1. Continue with 2.

## Mussels or Sausages in Bacon Rolls

*36 tinned or smoked mussels,*
*well-drained (approximately*
*225 g, 8 oz), or 36 cocktail*
*sausages*

*12 rashers thin bacon*
*(approximately 170 g, 6 oz)*
*mustard if using sausages,*
*optional*

1. Cut each rasher of bacon into 3, and stretch each piece lengthwise. If using sausages spread bacon with mustard. Wrap each mussel or sausage in the bacon, and either secure with a stick or pack so close that they cannot unroll.
2. Bake in the oven at 200°C (400°F) for 7 minutes. Serve hot on sticks.

Suitable for freezing after completing 1. Continue with 2. May be prepared in advance to the end of 1. Continue with 2.

## Chicken Livers in Bacon Rolls

*36 pieces of chicken liver*
*(approximately 360 g, 13 oz)*

*12 rashers thin bacon*
*(approximately 170 g, 6 oz)*
*2 tablespoons oil*

1. Fry the chicken livers very gently in the oil for 2–3 minutes. Cut the rashers into 3 and stretch each piece lengthwise and wrap round the livers. (If you prefer the livers to be pink inside, omit the oil and the frying.)
2. Bake at 200°C (400°F) for 6 minutes.

Suitable for freezing and for preparing in advance as for Mussels in Bacon Rolls (above).

## Chicken in Bacon Rolls

*36 small pieces of cooked*
*chicken (approximately*
*120 g, 4½ oz)*

*145 g (5 oz) ready-sliced*
*processed gruyère*
*12 rashers thin bacon*
*(approximately 170 g, 6 oz)*

1. Cut the gruyère into 72 small pieces, and sandwich the chicken between the pieces, pressing firmly together. Cut the bacon rashers in 3, stretch lengthwise, and wrap them round the chicken and gruyère.

2. Bake at 200°C (400°F) for 7–8 minutes. Serve hot on sticks.

Suitable for freezing and for preparing in advance as for Mussels in Bacon Rolls (page 35).

## Stuffed Mushrooms

For the mushrooms:                 2½ tablespoons oil
36 fresh button mushrooms

For the stuffing:
30 g (1 oz) onion, finely          salt and pepper
  chopped or stalks from the       30 almonds, skinned and
  mushrooms, finely chopped          finely chopped, or 90 g (3 oz)
60 g (2 oz) butter                   shrimps or prawns, finely
2 rounded tablespoons fresh          chopped
  breadcrumbs                      1 tablespoon cream

1. Remove the stalks from the mushrooms to leave a hollow in the centre. Melt the butter in a pan, add the onion and simmer for 5–10 minutes till just soft. Add the mushroom stalks and continue to simmer a further 2–3 minutes. Add the breadcrumbs. Add the rest of the ingredients and mix well. Season. Allow to cool and stuff the mushrooms with the mixture until level with their tops.
2. Bake at 200°C (400°F) for 8–9 minutes. Serve at once.

Not suitable for freezing. May be prepared in advance to the end of 1. Continue with 2.

## Savoury Chestnuts

36 chestnuts, parboiled and        ¼ level teaspoon salt
  skinned carefully to keep        ¼ level teaspoon cayenne
  them whole                       45 g (1½ oz) melted butter
2 tablespoons parmesan             90 g (3 oz) fresh white
  cheese                             breadcrumbs

1. Boil the chestnuts for 10 minutes, turn off the heat, and remove a few chestnuts at a time for peeling, keep the rest in the hot water. Hold a chestnut in the left hand (if you are right-handed), wearing a glove, and cut a cross with a very sharp knife across the base of the chestnut. Still holding it in your gloved hand, peel off the skin, taking hold of it at the base when you have cut it. It should come off easily in four pieces, leaving the chestnut whole. It's advisable to boil a few extra, in case some crumble. Dip the chestnuts in hot, melted butter, then in the mixture of parmesan, salt and cayenne. Dip again in the butter, and then in the breadcrumbs.

2. Bake at 200° C (400° F) for 8 minutes, until beginning to brown. Or omit the breadcrumbs, and bake in the parmesan mixture only. Serve hot.

Not suitable for freezing. May be prepared in advance to the end of 1. Continue with 2.

## Chestnut Balls

For the balls:
*225 g (8 oz) chestnuts, parboiled and peeled (page 36)*

*60 g (2 oz) onion, chopped finely*
*30 g (1 oz) butter*
*1 medium egg, lightly beaten*
*salt and pepper*

For the dressing:
*see Stuffed Olive Balls, (page 41*

1. Simmer the onion in the butter till soft, and add the peeled chestnuts, and continue to simmer until the chestnuts are soft enough to fall to pieces. Season. Sieve, or pulverize in a blender, and add the egg.
2. Form the mixture into small balls, and dip in the flour, and in the egg mixture, and roll in the breadcrumbs.
3. Deep fry at 200° C (400° F) until well browned.

Suitable for freezing (see Deep Freezing of Meatballs, page 15). May be prepared in advance (a) to the end of 1. Continue with 2. Or (b) to the end of 2. To re-heat, bake in the oven at 200° C (400° F) for 4–5 minutes.

## Dolmades

*110 g (4 oz) minced lamb, or chicken livers, cut finely or minced*
*2 tablespoons olive oil*
*80 g (2½ oz) onion, finely chopped*
*110 g (4 oz) rice after boiling*

*60 g (2 oz) pine kernels*
*2 teaspoons parsley, finely chopped*
*1 teaspoon lemon juice*
*salt and pepper*
*36 vine leaves*
*½ pint chicken stock or water*

1. Fry the minced lamb for 2–3 minutes, or the chicken livers for 1 minute, add the chopped onion, and simmer till soft, with the lid on. Add the lemon juice, the cooked rice, the pine kernels and the parsley, and mix well. Season. Prepare the vine leaves. If they have

been stored in brine, soak them in hot water for a few minutes, then in cold water, and dry them. If fresh, plunge into boiling water for 2–3 minutes, then into cold, and dry them. Lay a teaspoon of the mixture near the base of each leaf, and fold the base over. Fold the sides over, and then roll firmly to the end of the leaf.

2. Lay, open side down, in a dish, with the bundles very close together, and pour the stock over. Cover the dish, and bake for ½ hour at 180°C (350°F), making sure that the stock never boils dry. Serve hot.

Suitable for freezing after completing 1. To cook, thaw for 1 hour and continue with 2. May be prepared in advance (a) to the end of 1. Continue with 2. Or (b) to the end of 2. Re-heat carefully over a ring, and simmer gently for 10 minutes until heated through.

## Herby Balls

For the balls:

*30 g (1 oz) onion, finely chopped or minced*
*30 g (1 oz) lean bacon, finely minced*
*20 g (¾ oz) butter or margarine*
*90 g (3 oz) fresh white breadcrumbs*

*½ tablespoon oil*
*1 tablespoon parsley*
*1 level teaspoon dried marjoram or thyme, or rounded teaspoon fresh*
*¾ level teaspoon salt*
*2 medium eggs, lightly beaten*

For the dressing:
*see recipe for Stuffed Olive Balls (page 41)*

1. Simmer the onion in the butter until soft. Add the bacon, and continue until cooked. Mix together all the ingredients.
2 and 3. As for Chestnut Balls (page 37).

Suitable for freezing and for preparing in advance (see Chestnut Balls, page 37).

## Soft Roes on Sticks

*180 g (6½ oz) soft roes*
*30 g (1 oz) butter*
*1½ tablespoons oil*
*2 teaspoons lemon juice*
*30 g (1 oz) flour*

*1 small egg mixed with 1 teaspoon water*
*90 g (3 oz) breadcrumbs*
*salt and black pepper*

Squeeze the lemon juice over the roes. Cut them into 36 pieces, in 2 cm (¾ in) cubes. Dip in the flour, the egg and water mixture and the breadcrumbs. Sprinkle with a little salt and black pepper and shallow fry in the butter and oil. Serve hot on sticks, with more lemon juice squeezed over if wished.

# 2(c). Meat and Fish Balls

**EACH RECIPE MAKES 36**

Hot          **Pork Meatballs**

For the meatballs:
*170 g (6 oz) pork, including
  some fat, finely minced
1 small clove garlic, crushed
15 g (½ oz) plain flour
30 g (1 oz) fresh breadcrumbs
1 medium egg, lightly beaten
1 tablespoon oil
½ level teaspoon salt
pepper*

For the dressing:
*30 g (1 oz) plain flour
1 medium egg mixed with 1
  teaspoon water
90 g (3 oz) fresh white
  breadcrumbs*

1. Mix all ingredients together until well blended. Shape into balls the size of small marbles.
2. Cover with flour, dip into the egg and water mixture, and roll in the breadcrumbs (see Egg and Breadcrumb Dressing, page 13).
3. Deep fry until well browned.

Suitable for freezing (see Deep Freezing of Meatballs, page 15). May be prepared in advance (a) to the end of 2. Continue with 3. Or (b) to the end of 3. Re-heat in the oven at 200° C (400° F) for 5–6 minutes.

Hot **Veal Fricadelles**

For the balls:

170 g (6 oz) lean veal, finely
  minced
30 g (1 oz) bacon, or bacon
  fat, finely minced
30 g (1 oz) onion, finely
  chopped
15 g (½ oz) butter or
  margarine
1 clove garlic, crushed
2 small tomatoes, skinned,
  de-seeded and chopped

¾ level teaspoon dried basil
  or thyme or tarragon, or 1½
  teaspoons if fresh
2–3 sprigs parsley, chopped
45 g (1½ oz) fresh white
  breadcrumbs
2 tablespoons stock
1 small egg, lightly beaten
1 level teaspoon salt
black pepper

For the dressing:

30 g (1 oz) plain flour              2 tablespoons oil for frying

1. Simmer the onion and garlic in the butter or margarine with the lid on till soft. Add the tomatoes, and simmer till the juice has almost evaporated. Add all the other ingredients and mix thoroughly till well blended. Shape into balls the size of small marbles.
2. Roll in the flour.
3. Shallow fry until browned.
4. Serve with Fresh Tomato Sauce (page 67) either as a dip or as a coating.

Suitable for freezing (see Deep Freezing of Meatballs, page 15). May be prepared in advance (see previous recipe).

Hot **Stuffed Olive Balls**

For the balls:

36 stuffed olives,
  approximately 110 g (4 oz)
36 small Meatballs (page 40)
  using 110 g (4 oz) uncooked
  pork

For the dressing:

1 medium egg mixed with 1
  teaspoon water
30 g (1 oz) plain flour
90 g (3 oz) fresh breadcrumbs

1. Slit down one side of each stuffed olive, open as wide as possible, and insert a meatball. Smooth the meat round so that half the olive is visible, and half the meat.
2. Dip each ball in the flour and in the egg and water mixture, and roll in the breadcrumbs.
3. Deep fry at 200°C (400°F) until browned. Serve hot on cocktail sticks.

Not suitable for freezing. May be prepared in advance (a) to the end of 2. Continue with 3. Or (b) to the end of 3. Re-heat in the oven at 200°C (400°F) for 4–5 minutes.


Hot                    **Chinese Meatballs**

For the meatballs:                For the dressing:
*310g (11oz) pork, finely*        *see recipe for Pork Meatballs*
*  minced*                        *  (page 40)*
*1 small clove garlic, crushed*
*1 dessertspoon soy sauce*
*½ level teaspoon salt*

Method as in recipe for Pork Meatballs (page 40).

Suitable for freezing (see Deep Freezing of Meatballs, page 15). May be prepared in advance (see recipe for Pork Meatballs, page 40).


Hot                    **Lebanese Meatballs**

For the balls:
*170g (6oz) lamb, finely*         *1 level teaspoon salt*
*  minced*                        *1 level teaspoon dried thyme,*
*1 clove garlic, crushed*         *  or 2 if fresh*
*60g (2oz) onion, finely*         *1 level teaspoon curry powder*
*  chopped or minced*             *½ level teaspoon allspice*
*60g (2oz) pine kernels*          *¼ level teaspoon black pepper*
*1 small egg, lightly beaten*     *1 tablespoon olive oil*
*2–3 sprigs parsley, chopped*

For the dressing:
*see recipe for Veal Fricadelles*
*  (page 41)*

1. Fry the pine kernels gently in the olive oil, until beginning to brown. Mix with all the other ingredients, until well blended. Shape into balls the size of small marbles.
2. and 3. As in the recipe for Veal Fricadelles, (page 41). The pine kernels make it difficult to roll tidy balls, but this is of no importance as it adds to the appearance of the meatballs to have the nuts sticking out in all directions.

Suitable for freezing (see Deep Freezing of Meatballs, page 15). May be prepared in advance (see recipe for Pork Meatballs, page 40).

Cold                    **Curried Meatballs**

For the meatballs:
*170 g (6 oz) beef, minced finely*     *1 tablespoon oil*
*45 g (1½ oz) onion, minced*           *1 level tablespoon normal*
*finely*                                 *strength curry powder*
*1 clove garlic, crushed*              *1 small egg, lightly beaten*
*45 g (1½ oz) mushrooms,*              *¾ level teaspoon salt*
*chopped finely*

For the dressing:
*see recipe for Pork Meatballs*
*(page 40), or Veal Fricadelles*
*(page 41)*

1. Sauté the mushrooms in the oil, mix with all the other ingredients and blend thoroughly. Shape into balls the size of small marbles.
2. and 3. As in recipe for Pork Meatballs (page 40) or Veal Fricadelles (page 41). Serve with Basic Creamy Dip (page 72).

Suitable for freezing (see Deep Freezing of Meatballs, page 15). May be prepared in advance (see recipe for Pork Meatballs, page 40).


Hot               **Chicken Balls with Pistachios**

For the balls:
*110 g (4 oz) chicken, cooked*         *1 dessertspoon olive oil*
*and minced*                           *1 teaspoon lemon juice*
*60 g (2 oz) fresh white*              *salt and pepper*
*breadcrumbs*                          *juice of half a lemon to*
*1 tablespoon chicken stock*            *squeeze over the meatballs*
*30 g (1 oz) pistachio nuts,*           *just before serving*
*chopped finely*

For the dressing:
*see recipe for Pork Meatballs*
*(page 40), or Veal Fricadelles*
*(page 41)*

Method as for Pork Meatballs (page 40).

Suitable for freezing (see Deep Freezing of Meatballs, page 15). May be prepared in advance (see recipe for Pork Meatballs, page 40).

Hot **Moroccan Kofta**

For the kofta:
*285 g (10 oz) lamb, including
some fat, finely minced
90 g (3 oz) onion, finely
chopped or minced
5 fresh mint leaves, chopped
2–3 sprigs parsley, chopped
½ level teaspoon dried
marjoram*

*1 level teaspoon salt
½ level teaspoon black pepper
generous pinches of cumin,
cayenne pepper, paprika,
ginger and cardamon, or
make up ½ level teaspoon of
whichever of these spices
are available*

For the dressing:
*see recipe for Veal Fricadelles
(page 41) using olive oil*

Mix all ingredients together until well blended. Shape into balls the size of small marbles, roll in the flour and shallow fry.

Suitable for freezing (see Deep Freezing of Meatballs, page 15). May be prepared in advance (see recipe for Pork Meatballs, page 40).

Hot or cold **Swedish Meatballs**

For the meatballs:
*170 g (6 oz) finely minced veal
or, alternatively; 90 g (3 oz)
beef, finely minced, and 45 g
(1½ oz) pork, finely minced,
and 45 g (1½ oz) veal, finely
minced
90 g (3 oz) onion, finely
chopped or minced*

*20 g (¾ oz) butter or
margarine
45 g (1½ oz) fresh white
breadcrumbs
3 tablespoons thin cream
1 small egg, lightly beaten
1 teaspoon parsley, chopped
¾ level teaspoon salt
black pepper*

For the dressing:
*see recipe for Veal Fricadelles
(page 41)*

Method as previous recipe. Serve with the sour cream dip (page 75).

Suitable for freezing (see Deep Freezing of Meatballs, page 15). May be prepared in advance (see recipe for Pork Meatballs, page 40).

Hot or cold          **Sausagemeat Balls**

For the meatballs:
*170 g (6 oz) sausagemeat*
*6 teaspoons tableready*
  *horseradish sauce, or 3*
  *tablespoons Dijon mustard,*
  *optional*
*salt and pepper*

For the dressing:
*see recipe for Veal Fricadelles*
  *(page 41)*

(Use only good quality sausagemeat. This varies in flavour, so fry one meatball first, and then adjust the seasoning.)

Shape into balls the size of small marbles, roll in the flour and fry in the shallow fat until well browned, allowing time for the meat to cook in the centre. Serve in a sauce or with a dip.

Suitable for freezing (see Deep Freezing of Meatballs, page 15). May be prepared in advance (see recipe for Pork Meatballs, page 40).

Hot      **Sausagemeat Balls with Cheese Centres**

For the balls:
*270 g (9½ oz) sausagemeat*
*90 g (3 oz) gruyère or*
  *emmenthal cheese, cut into*
  *36 cubes*
*salt and pepper*

For the dressing:
*see recipe for Stuffed Olive*
  *Balls (page 41)*

1. Wrap the sausagemeat in a very thin layer round the cubes of cheese, using as little as possible.
2. Shape into small balls. Dip the balls in the flour, in the egg mixture, and roll in the breadcrumbs, pressing them firmly in.
3. Deep fry at 200°C (400°F) until well browned.

Suitable for freezing (see Deep Freezing of Meatballs, page 15). May be prepared in advance (a) to the end of 1. Continue with 2. Or (b) to the end of 3. Reheat in the oven at 200°C (400°F) for 4–5 minutes.

Cold          **Ham and Egg Balls**

For the balls:
*4 small eggs, hard-boiled*
*1 tablespoon Mayonnaise*
  *(page 69)*
*110 g (4 oz) minced ham*
*1 teaspoon parsley or chives*
*salt and black pepper*

For the covering:
*see recipe for Cheese Marbles*
  *(page 26)*

Mash the yolks of the eggs with the mayonnaise, the parsley or chives and the minced ham. Chop the whites of the eggs, and add to the mixture. Add the salt and pepper as needed. Roll in the selected covering.

Not suitable for freezing. May be prepared a few hours in advance and kept cool.


Hot                         **Fishballs**

For the fishballs:

*225 g (8 oz) white fish or salmon, filleted*

*12 tablespoons fish stock or milk*

*45 g (1½ oz) butter or margarine*

*45 g (1½ oz) plain flour*

*3 tablespoons thin cream*

*salt and pepper*

For the dressing:
*see recipe for Pork Meatballs (page 40)*

1. Simmer the fish in the stock or milk until just cooked. Remove from the stock, and mash. Add the cream to the remaining stock, and make up the quantity to 12 tablespoons again, by adding more milk or stock if necessary. Make a white sauce from the flour, butter and stock mixture (page 68). Add the fish and seasoning, and blend thoroughly. Refrigerate till cold. Shape into balls the size of small marbles.
2. and 3. As in the recipe for Pork Meatballs (page 40). Serve with Chilli Sauce (page 67) as a dip.

Suitable for freezing (see Deep Freezing of Meatballs, page 15). May be prepared in advance (see recipe for Pork Meatballs, page 40).


Hot                         **Shellfish Balls**

For the fishballs:

*90 g (3 oz) lobster, crab, or prawns, or a mixture of these with white fish, cooked and chopped*

*60 g (2 oz) onion, finely chopped or minced*

*15 g (½ oz) butter*

*45 g (1½ oz) fresh white breadcrumbs*

*a tablespoon liquid from simmered shells, or from a tin, or thin cream*

*1–2 sprigs parsley, chopped*

*pinch dried thyme*

*juice and finely grated rind of ½ lemon*

*¼ level teaspoon salt*

*white pepper*

For the dressing:
*see recipe for Pork Meatballs*
 *(page 40)*

1. Simmer the onions in the butter until soft, and mix with all the
other ingredients, till well blended. Shape into balls the size of small
marbles.
2. and 3. As in the recipe for Pork Meatballs (page 40).

Suitable for freezing (see Deep Freezing of Meatballs, page 15). May
be prepared in advance (see recipe for Pork Meatballs, page 40).

Hot          **Chinese Fishballs**

For the fishballs:

*90 g (3 oz) lobster, crab or*
 *prawns*
*90 g (3 oz) white fish, filleted,*
 *and cooked in a little stock*
 *or milk*
*45 g (1½ oz) pork, finely*
 *minced*

*1 teaspoon cornflour*
*2 teaspoons dry sherry, in*
 *place of sake*
*2 teaspoons soy sauce*
*1 small egg*
*¼ teaspoon salt*
*pinch cayenne*

For the dressing:
*see the recipe for batter (page*
 *61)*

1. Mix all ingredients together and shape into balls the size of small
marbles.
2. Dip the balls in the batter, and deep fry at 200°C (400°F) until
browned.

Suitable for freezing (a) after completing 1. Thaw for 30 minutes and
continue with 2 (see Deep Freezing, page 15). Or after completing 2.
To re-heat, bake in the oven at 200°C (400°F) for 5–6 minutes. May
be prepared in advance to the end of 1. Continue with 2. Or to the end
of 2. Re-heat in the oven at 200°C (400°F) for 5–6 minutes.

Hot or Cold **Salmon and Cream Cheese Balls**

For the balls:

*90 g (3 oz) soft cream cheese*
*90 g (3 oz) salmon, cooked*
 *and flaked*

*1½ teaspoons parsley,*
 *chopped*
*45 g (1½ oz) fresh white*
 *breadcrumbs*

For the dressing:
*see recipe for Stuffed Olive*
 *Balls (page 41)*

Mix the ingredients together, and shape into small balls. Roll in the flour, dip in the egg and water mixture, and cover in breadcrumbs. Deep fry until browned. Serve hot or cold.

Not suitable for freezing. May be prepared in advance if serving cold. If serving hot, re-heat in the oven at 200° C (400° F) for 4–5 minutes.

Hot                    **Anchovy and Herb Balls**

For the balls:
*6 large anchovy fillets in oil*
*75 g (2½ oz) fresh white*
 *breadcrumbs*
*15 g (½ oz) fat bacon, or pork*
 *fat, finely minced*
*110 g (4 oz) onion, finely*
 *chopped or minced*
*30 g (1 oz) butter or margarine*

*1 level tablespoon parsley,*
 *chopped*
*1 level tablespoon fresh*
 *thyme, chopped, or ½ level*
 *tablespoon if dried*
*1 tablespoon orange juice, or*
 *stock, or milk*
*1 medium egg, lightly beaten*

For the dressing:
*see recipe for Stuffed Olive*
 *Balls (page 41)*

Chop or mince the anchovies, and mix all ingredients together until well blended. Shape into small balls. Roll in the flour, dip in the egg mixture and cover with the breadcrumbs. Deep fry till well browned. Serve with a Basic Creamy Dip (page 72), or with Fresh Tomato Sauce (page 67) used as a dip.

Suitable for freezing (see Deep Freezing of Meatballs, page 15). May be prepared in advance, and re-heated in the oven at 200° C (400° F) for 4–5 minutes.

# 2(d). Hot Baby Kebabs

**EACH RECIPE MAKES 36 KEBABS**

## Baby Kebabs

Select from the following enough items to fill 36 cocktail sticks, allowing an average of 4 per stick:

small cocktail sausages or pieces of sausage
single leaves of onions, cut in suitable sizes
pieces of green or sweet pepper
cubes of gruyère or emmenthal cheese
pieces of very firm tomato, with skin, or wrap the tomato in very thin pieces of bacon rasher
small whole mushrooms, with the stem cut flat
cubes of apple, dipped in oil and brown sugar
sections of pineapple
dates or prunes, cut in half lengthwise, wrapped in bacon (pages 33–4)
small pieces of chicken liver, wrapped in bacon (page 35)
thin rashers of bacon, rolled up
meatballs (page 40)
raw chicken breast, veal or lamb, beef or pork fillet, allowing 3 cubes to 10 g (⅓ oz)
cubes of aubergine or courgette, allowing 10 cubes to 30 g (1 oz)
cubes of ham
bayleaves, to give flavour
cubes of bread, rubbed in garlic

METHOD (1)
Make a suitable selection, e.g. cubes of pork, sections of pineapple, prunes in bacon, and pieces of green sweet pepper, and marinate in oil for 30 minutes. There is no need to marinate anything wrapped in

bacon. Place on the cocktail sticks and bake in the oven at 200° C (400° F) for 6–10 minutes, according to ingredients. Pour over a very little sauce, e.g. Chilli Sauce (page 67), before serving, or serve with a dip (pages 71–75).

METHOD (2)
As in Method (1) but pour over a little sauce before cooking.

METHOD (3)
Place several of the same item on one stick, e.g. 3 mushrooms in bacon, but keep each item very small.

METHOD (4)
Cook the ingredients first, and thread on afterwards, e.g. chicken livers in bacon, mushrooms and onion leaves. Sprinkle with bread-crumbs and bake in the oven at 250° C (480° F) for a further 2–3 minutes to brown the crumbs.

Some suggestions:

## English Kebabs

*A Mixed Grill*:
Use cubes of beef, lamb, kidney, bacon and mushrooms.
    Marinate in 3 level teaspoons tomato ketchup, 3 teaspoons wine vinegar or lemon juice, a pinch of cayenne pepper, a pinch of salt, 3 level teaspoons made English mustard, and 12 teaspoons oil. For a sweeter marinade, dissolve 1 rounded teaspoon brown sugar in 3 teaspoons Worcestershire sauce, and add to the above.

Use alternate cubes of pork with small pieces of prune.
    Marinate in 3 tablespoons oil, 1 tablespoon lemon juice, 1 crushed clove garlic, and pinches of thyme and sage.

## Greek or Middle Eastern Kebabs

Use cubes of lamb with quartered tomatoes, pieces of onion and red sweet peppers.
    Marinate in 4 tablespoons olive oil, juice of 1 small lemon, ½ level teaspoon cinnamon, pinch of salt and black pepper.

Use cubes of veal instead of lamb.
    Marinate in 4 tablespoons olive oil, juice of ¼ lemon, slices of onion, a bay leaf, 1 level teaspoon marjoram or Italian oregano, or thyme or rosemary.

## Italian Kebabs

Use alternate cubes of beef with small mushrooms, and one small bayleaf. Serve with Fresh Tomato Sauce (page 67).
Marinate in 2 tablespoons olive oil, 1 clove crushed garlic, ¼ teaspoon oregano.

Use tiny pieces of thin ham (40 g, 1⅓ oz makes 36 pieces), cubes of veal, leaves of onion, and small squares of bread rubbed in garlic.
Marinate in a little olive oil.

Use cubes of veal, aubergine and courgette. Sprinkle salt on the aubergine and leave to soak for 1 hour, press dry with a cloth or absorbent paper.
Marinate the veal, courgettes and aubergines in 4 tablespoons olive oil. Thread on cocktail sticks, roll in breadcrumbs, and bake for 15 minutes at 200° C (400° F), adding more oil if they seem too dry. Or, dip each piece in egg and breadcrumb, and deep fry first. Then thread and re-heat for 2–3 minutes in the oven. Serve with a little Fresh Tomato Sauce (page 67) poured over.

## French Kebabs

Use cubes of lamb alternating with cubes of pork and one small bayleaf.
Marinate in 2 tablespoons white wine, 2 tablespoons olive oil, 1 clove garlic, crushed, and fresh herbs as available.

Use cubes of beef, button mushrooms, green sweet peppers cut in 2½ cm (1 in) squares.
Marinate in 2 tablespoons red wine, 2 tablespoons olive oil, 1 teaspoon lemon juice, 1 teaspoon soy sauce, 1 clove garlic crushed, ¼ teaspoon Dijon mustard, pinch thyme and a little sliced onion.

Use pieces of lamb, green sweet peppers, onion leaves, quartered tomatoes.
Marinate in 2 tablespoons olive oil, 1 tablespoon lemon juice, 1 teaspoon liquid honey well dissolved in the lemon juice, 1 clove garlic, crushed, and 2 bayleaves, salt and pepper.

## Chinese Kebabs

Use cubes of pork alone:
Marinate in 2 tablespoons sweet sherry, 2 tablespoons oil, and a pinch salt; or
Marinate in 2 tablespoons soy sauce, 2 teaspoons liquid honey well dissolved in 2 tablespoons dry sherry to take the place of sake,

and chopped spring onions. Sprinkle soy sauce on after cooking, or serve in a mustard sauce; or

Marinate in a sweet sour sauce of 30 g (1 oz) brown sugar, 1½ tablespoons wine vinegar, 1 tablespoon soy sauce, 1 tablespoon oil, 1 tablespoon water. Dissolve the sugar in the water first.

## Indonesian Kebabs

Use cubes of pork alone:

Marinate in 2 tablespoons soy sauce, 2 tablespoons lemon juice, ⅛ teaspoon powdered ginger, 1 teaspoon cumin, 1 spring onion chopped, 1 teaspoon brown sugar, pinch of salt and black pepper.

# 2(e). Hot Cheese Savouries

**EACH RECIPE MAKES 36 SAVOURIES**

## Baby Welsh Rarebits

*60 g (2 oz) butter or margarine*
*120 g (4 oz) grated cheddar*
*2 tablespoons milk*
*½ teaspoon Worcestershire*
  *sauce*

*1 teaspoon made English*
  *mustard*
*pinch salt and pinch cayenne*
  *pepper*

1. Mix all ingredients together and blend thoroughly.
2. Spread over 4 average slices of bread (approximately 11½ cm, 4½ in square), and cut each slice into 9 squares.
3. Bake at 225°C (450°F) for 6 minutes.

Suitable for freezing after completing 2 (see Deep Freezing page 15). To cook, place on a baking tray while still frozen, and thaw for 30 minutes. Continue with 3. May be prepared in advance to the end of 2. Continue with 3.

## Parmesan Crostini

*4 large slices of bread, crusts*
  *removed*

*60 g (2 oz) parmesan cheese,*
  *finely grated*
*60 g (2 oz) butter*

1. Cut each slice of bread into 9 canapés; melt the butter in a pan, dip the canapés into the warm butter, on both sides, and place on a baking tray. Sprinkle the parmesan cheese over them.
2. Bake at 200°C (400°F) for 4–5 minutes, until just crisp. Serve hot, at once.

Suitable for freezing after completing 1. To cook, place on a baking tray while still frozen and leave for 30 minutes to thaw. Continue from 2. May be prepared in advance to the end of 1. Continue with 2.

## Cheddar or Gruyère Crostini

4 large slices of bread, crusts removed
90 g (3 oz) cheddar or gruyère cheese

12 small or 9 large anchovies (and the oil from the tin), or thin slices of tomato or olives
45 g (1½ oz) butter

1. Cut each slice of bread into 8 or 10 rectangles, approximately 2½ by 5 cm (1 in by 2 in). Melt the butter in a pan, and dip the slices of bread in the butter, on one side only. Alternatively, spread softened butter over the bread. Place, buttered side downwards, on a baking tray. Cut the cheese very thinly indeed, if possible with a cheese slicer, and lay the pieces over each piece of bread. Cut the anchovies diagonally lengthwise, to make 36 pieces, and lay these diagonally across each crostini. Pour over the oil from the tin. (Or place tomato, or olive slices on top.)
2. Bake in the oven at 200°C (400°F) for 5–6 minutes.

Not suitable for freezing; the cheese falls off the bread too easily, so it is not worth the trouble. May be prepared in advance to the end of 1.

## Cheese and Almond Croutons

36 bread croutons
140 g (5 oz) grated cheddar cheese
75 g (2½ oz) margarine or butter

2 tablespoons chopped almonds
6 pinches paprika

1. Blend the cheese and butter or margarine together, and spread over the croutons. Sprinkle with the chopped almonds and a very little paprika.
2. Bake at 200°C (400°F) for 6 minutes.

Suitable for freezing after completing 1. To thaw, place on baking tray for 20 minutes, and continue with 2. May be prepared in advance to the end of 1. Continue with 2.

## Camembert Croquettes

For the croquettes:
*45 g (1½ oz) plain flour*
*45 g (1½ oz) butter*
*3 dl (½ pint) milk*

*1 camembert cheese*
*1 egg yolk*
*pinch salt and pinch cayenne*

For the dressing:
*see recipe for Pork Meatballs*
*(page 40)*

1. Make a white sauce from the butter, flour, milk and seasonings, (page 68). Remove the skin from the camembert, and sieve into the sauce. Add the egg yolk. Leave in the refrigerator to cool. When quite cold, roll in the flour, egg and water mixture and breadcrumbs (see Egg and Breadcrumb Dressing – white sauce base, page 14). Refrigerate again until cold.
2. Deep fry at 200° C (400° F) until golden brown.

Suitable for freezing (a) after completing 1 (see Deep Freezing for Meatballs, page 15). To cook, place on a baking tray to thaw for 30 minutes, and continue with 2. Or, (b) after completing 2. Thaw as above, and bake in the oven at 200° C (400° F) for 5–6 minutes. May be prepared in advance to the end of 1. Continue with 2. Or to the end of 2. Re-heat at 200° C (400° F) for 5–6 minutes.

## Gruyère Balls

For the balls:
*35 g (1¼ oz) butter or*
  *margarine*
*35 g (1¼ oz) plain flour*
*2 dl (⅓ pint) milk*
*1 small egg yolk*

*120 g (4 oz) gruyère or*
  *emmenthal cheese, grated*
*1 level teaspoon salt*
*pinch white pepper*
*pinch cayenne*

For the dressing:
*see recipe for Pork Meatballs*
*(page 40)*

1. Make a white sauce with the butter, flour and milk (page 68). Add the egg yolk and the grated cheese, beat well together, and season. Leave in the refrigerator to cool. When quite cold, roll in the flour, egg and water mixture, and breadcrumbs (see Egg and Breadcrumb Dressing – white sauce base, page 14).
Refrigerate again until very cold.
2. Deep fry at 200° C (400° F) until golden brown.

Suitable for freezing or preparing in advance (see previous recipe).

## Cheddar Cheese Balls

For the balls:
*45 g (1½ oz) plain flour*          *2 egg whites*
*170 g (6 oz) gruyère,*             *2 egg yolks*
  *emmenthal, or cheddar*          *pinch salt and pinch cayenne*
  *cheese, finely grated*            *pepper*

For the dressing:
*see recipe for Pork Meatballs*
  *(page 40) adding 30 g (1 oz)*
  *chopped toasted almonds*

1. Mix the flour, cheese, egg yolks and seasoning together. Beat the egg whites till stiff, and add just before frying. Roll the balls to the size of small marbles, and dip in the flour, the egg and water mixture, and the breadcrumbs mixed with the almonds.
2. Deep fry at 200°C (400°F).

Suitable for freezing (a) after completing 1. To cook, thaw on a baking tray for 30 minutes and continue with 2. Or (b) after 2. Thaw as above, and re-heat in the oven at 200°C (400°F) for 5–6 minutes. May be prepared in advance (a) to the end of 1. Continue with 2. Or (b) to the end of 2. Re-heat at 200°C (400°F) for 5–6 minutes.


## Cheese Brochettes

*120 g (4 oz) cheddar or*          *30 g (1 oz) plain flour*
  *gruyère cheese*                  *1 large egg, lightly beaten*
*12 very thin rashers bacon*        *90 g (3 oz) fresh white*
  *(approximately 170 g, 6 oz)*      *breadcrumbs*

1. Cut the bacon rashers into three pieces each, and stretch them lengthwise. Cut the cheese into 36 cubes. Wrap the bacon round the cubes of cheese, and place at the end of a cocktail stick. Dip them into the flour, the beaten egg and then in the breadcrumbs.
2. Heat enough fat in a pan to produce a depth of about 2½ cm (1 in). Place the brochettes, with the stick standing upright, in the fat, and fry till the bacon is crisp and the cheese beginning to melt.

Suitable for freezing after completing 1. Thaw for 30 minutes, and continue with it. May also be prepared in advance in the same way.

## Bel Paese Fritters

1 bel paese cheese, weighing
180 g (6 oz)

For the dressing:
*see recipe for Pork Meatballs*
*(page 40), or batter mixture*
*(page 61)*

1. Remove the outer covering of the cheese, and cut into four quarters. Cut each quarter into 9 wedges, like slices of cake, making 36 in all. Cut each wedge in half, downwards across the slice, giving a thick and a thin end. Reverse the thin end and place it on top of the thick end, in order to make it into an evenly shaped rectangle. This makes it more manageable.
2. Dip in the flour, the egg and water mixture, and the breadcrumbs, or into the batter.
3. Deep fry till well browned.

Suitable for freezing. If using breadcrumbs, complete 2 and then freeze. Thaw for 30 minutes and continue with 3. If using batter, complete 1. Thaw and continue with 2 and 3. May be prepared in advance in the same way.

## Processed Gruyère Savouries

Processed gruyère is easier to use than real gruyère as it will not go chewy or stringy when baked, as gruyère is liable to do. It is better to use real gruyère only when it is grated, and mixed with other ingredients.

1. Cut 255 g (9 oz) processed gruyère into 36 small cubes. Dip in 30 g (1 oz) plain flour, 1 large egg lightly beaten, and 90 g (3 oz) fresh white breadcrumbs. Deep fry. Serve on cocktail sticks.
2. Cut 90 g (3 oz) processed gruyère into 72 small slivers, 3 cm by 1½ cm (1¼ in by ½ in). Cut 36 small pieces of ham (90 g 3 oz) and sandwich each piece of ham between two pieces of gruyère. Dip in the flour, egg and breadcrumbs, as in 1, and deep fry. Serve on cocktail sticks.
3. Prepare the cheese and ham as in 2, and sandwich these between thin slices of bread, cut to the same size. Dip in 2 large eggs, lightly beaten, and shallow fry.
4. Prepare 36 bread bases, as in the recipe for Parmesan Crostini (page 53). On each spread a little anchovy paste, and lay a sliver of cheese on each (45 g, 1½ oz). Bake at 200° C (400° F) for 5 minutes. Sprinkle with parsley.
5. As in 4, but instead of the anchovy paste, lay a thin slice of tomato over, and bake.

6. As in 4, but instead of the anchovy paste, lay a small piece of anchovy over, and bake.

7. Prepare cubes of cheese as in 1, or 'sandwiches' of cheese and ham as in 2, dip in batter (page 61) and deep fry.


## Cheese with Asparagus

For the canapés:
*4 large slices of bread, with crusts removed*
*36 asparagus tips, or sections of stem*
*45 g (1½ oz) butter*

For the sauce:
*30 g (1 oz) butter or margarine*
*6 tablespoons milk*
*dash of Worcestershire sauce*
*170 g (6 oz) processed gruyère*
*pinch salt and pinch cayenne pepper*

1. Prepare the bases as for Cheddar and Gruyère Crostini (page 54). Lay an asparagus tip on each base.

2. Prepare the sauce by melting the butter with the milk and the Worcestershire sauce and seasoning. Add the processed gruyère in small pieces, and, keeping the heat very low, stir till it has melted. While still warm pour over the asparagus. Bake at 200° C (400° F) for 7–8 minutes. Serve at once.

Not suitable for freezing. May be prepared in advance to the end of 1.


## Aigrettes

*35 g (1¼ oz) butter*
*5 tablespoons water*
*75 g (2½ oz) plain flour*
*75 g (2½ oz) cheddar, grated*

*1 large egg*
*pinch salt and pinch cayenne*
*¼ teaspoon made mustard*
*35 g (1¼ oz) ham, optional*

1. Melt the butter with the water in the pan. Add the flour, all at once, and beat till the mixture comes cleanly away from the sides. (This takes only a minute.) Remove, cool a little, and beat in the egg first, then the cheese, salt, mustard and cayenne. Add the ham if using it.

2. Take up teaspoonfuls, and drop into deep fat, till well browned. Serve at once.

Suitable for freezing after completing 1 (see Deep Freezing of Meatballs, page 15). To cook, thaw in the containers for 2–3 hours, and continue with 2. May be prepared in advance in the same way.

## Cheese and Parsley Fritters

*45 g (1½ oz) semolina*
*1½ dl (¼ pint) milk*
*45 g (1½ oz) grated cheddar*
*½ egg, lightly beaten*
*2 teaspoons parsley, chopped*

*pinch salt and pinch cayenne*
*30 g (1 oz) plain flour*
*1 large egg, beaten*
*90 g (3 oz) fresh white*
  *breadcrumbs*

1. Simmer the semolina and milk together till they become very thick. Continue simmering very gently 2–3 minutes, stirring all the time. Take the pan off the heat and beat in the cheese, egg and seasonings and parsley. Tip the mixture out onto a wet dish, and spread it out evenly with a wet knife, to a depth of about 1¼ cm (½ in). Leave to cool. When cold, cut into 36 cubes. Dip them in flour, in the beaten egg and in the breadcrumbs (see Egg and Breadcrumb Dressing, page 13).
2. Deep fry for about 30 seconds only.

Suitable for freezing (a) after completing 1 (see Deep Freezing, page 15). To cook, thaw on a baking tray for 30 minutes, and continue with 2. Or, (b) after completing 2. To re-heat, thaw and bake in the oven at 200°C (400°F) for 6 minutes. May be prepared in advance in the same way.

## Cheese and Potato Gnocci

For the gnocci:
*335 g (12 oz) potatoes before*
  *peeling*
*90 g (3 oz) plain flour*
*1 medium egg, lightly beaten*
*30 g (1 oz) parmesan, grated*

*4 teaspoons parsley, chopped*
*2 teaspoons chives, chopped,*
  *or other fresh herbs*
*¼ level teaspoon salt*

For the dressing:
*30 g (1 oz) parmesan cheese,*
  *grated*

*30 g (1 oz) butter*

1. Boil the potatoes in salted water, and peel. While still hot put through a ricer or sieve, add the flour gradually, beating all the time, the beaten egg, parmesan, herbs and salt.
2. Turn out onto a floured board and knead till smooth. Divide into three balls for easier handling. Roll each piece into a long sausage shape, 2 cm (¾ in) in diameter, and 30 cm (12 in) long. Divide this with a knife into 12 pieces, giving 36 pieces in all.
3. Bring a large pan of water to the boil, slightly salted, and drop the gnocci in, a few at a time. Make sure the water remains just on the boil, but it must never boil furiously. Cook for 1 minute after they rise

to the surface. Remove with a slotted spoon, and lay in a buttered dish. Sprinkle at once with parmesan and butter, and leave in a hot oven to crisp slightly. Serve on cocktail sticks, with a hot Fresh Tomato Sauce (page 67).

Suitable for freezing (a) after completing 1. To cook, thaw in the container for 2–3 hours, and continue with 2 and 3. Or (b) after completing 2 (see Deep Freezing, page 15). To cook, thaw on a baking tray for 30 minutes, and then continue with 3.

## Cheese and Potato Scones

For the dough:
*125 g (4½ oz) potato, freshly boiled and mashed*
*75 g (2½ oz) plain flour*
*1½ level teaspoons baking powder*
*½ large egg, lightly beaten*

*45 g (1½ oz) butter, melted*
*45 g (1½ oz) cheddar cheese, grated finely*
*pinch dry mustard*
*pinch cayenne pepper*
*¼ level teaspoon salt*

For the filling:
*grated cheese, or pre-cooked bacon, finely chopped, or butter only, and double the quantity of cheese in the recipe*

1. Sift the flour and add the baking powder and seasoning. Mix in the potato, egg, melted butter and cheese. Knead into a ball, sprinkle on a little extra flour, remove from the bowl and divide into two balls. Shape each ball into a sausage approximately 30 cm (12 in) long, and then roll to approximately 30 cm by 10 cm (12 in by 4 in). Using a 5 cm (2 in) cutter, make 12 circles from each piece of dough. Gather the unused pieces, knead together, and re-roll, cutting 12 more circles.
2. Heat a griddle or flat frying pan to a medium heat, and cook the scones, with no added fat, till small brown patches appear. Turn over and repeat.
3. Sprinkle with filling, and allow time for the filling to heat before rolling up and skewering with cocktail sticks. Serve hot, at once.

Suitable for freezing after 2. Re-heat on the griddle or in the oven for 2–3 minutes, and continue with 3. May be prepared in advance and re-heated in the same way.

# 2(f). Beignets

**EACH RECIPE MAKES 36**

## Vegetable Beignets

Batter mixture:
*90 g (3 oz) cornflour*                     *white of 1 large or 2 small*
*little over 2 tablespoons oil*              *eggs*
*6 tablespoons water*

Mix together the cornflour, oil and water, and leave to rest for at least
2 hours. Fold in the stiffly beaten egg white just before use. Dip the
prepared vegetables in enough batter to cover with a thin layer and
deep fry at 200° C (400° F) until well browned.

*Aubergines*: Cut into 2 cm (¾ in) cubes, sprinkle with salt and leave
for at least 30 minutes. Press dry with a cloth or absorbent paper.
Replace the oil in the batter mixture with olive oil

*Beetroot*: Cook whole in its skin until just tender, using only small
roots, for about 1 hour. Cut into fingers 5 cm (2 in) long

*Carrots*: Use young carrots, cut into 2½ cm (1 in) pieces, and blanch
for 3 minutes

*Cauliflower*: Cut into florets and blanch for 2–3 minutes in salted
boiling water

*Celeriac*: Cut into fingers approximately 5 cm (2 in) long, and blanch
for 1 minute

*Courgettes*: Cut into sections approximately 2 cm (¾ in) square, and
blanch for 1 minute

*Mushrooms*: Sprinkle a little salt into the centre of each mushroom.
Do not blanch

Serve very hot, on sticks, with Barbecue Sauce (page 66), or Tartare Sauce (page 69) as a dip.

Suitable for freezing (see Deep Freezing, page 15). To re-heat, place the frozen beignets on a baking tray, thaw for 30 minutes, and bake in the oven at 240°C (460°F) for 5–6 minutes. May be prepared in advance and re-heated at 240°C (460°F) for 5–6 minutes.

### Prawn Fritters

*36 prawns (approximately 210g, 7oz, after removing shells)*      *batter mixture (page 61)*

As for Vegetable Beignets (page 61).

Suitable for freezing, and for preparing in advance, as for vegetable beignets.

### Mussel Fritters

*36 large mussels (approximately 225g, 8oz without shells)*      *batter mixture (page 61)*

As for Vegetable Beignets (page 61).

Not suitable for freezing or preparing in advance.

### Fritto Misto

*36 pieces of fish or shellfish (prawns, mussels, plaice or any other white fish, Fishballs (page 46) or Shellfish Balls (page 46)*      *batter mixture (page 61)*

Prepare the prawns and mussels as in the previous recipes. Cut the fish into strips 5–7 cm (2–3 in) long, and prepare the Fishballs (page 46) and Shellfish Balls (page 46). Dip in the batter and deep fry. Place all together on a dish garnished with wedges of lemon, and sprigs of parsley or watercress. Serve very hot, with cocktail sticks, and a selection of dips.

Suitable for freezing, with the exception of the mussels (see Vegetable Beignets, page 61). May also be prepared in advance.

## Pineapple Kromeskis

*36 small pieces of pineapple,
cut from 3 average rings*

*12 rashers very thin bacon
(140 g, 5 oz)
batter mixture (page 61)*

Cut each bacon rasher into 3 and stretch lengthwise. Wrap each piece of pineapple in the bacon and dip in the batter. There is no need to secure with a stick, as the batter will seal the contents as soon as it enters the hot fat. Deep fry at 200° C (400° F) until browned. Serve hot on cocktail sticks.

Suitable for freezing (see Vegetable Beignets, page 61). May also be prepared in advance.

## Cheese Kromeskis

*170 g (6 oz) gruyère or
emmenthal cheese, cut into
36 rectangles, the same
width as the bacon*

*12 rashers very thin bacon
(140 g, 5 oz)
batter mixture (page 61)*

Method, freezing and preparing in advance, as for Pineapple Kromeskis (above).

## Egg Kromeskis

For the basic sauce:
*20 g (¾ oz) butter or
margarine
20 g (¾ oz) plain flour
1½ dl (¼ pint) milk
½ egg yolk
30 g (1 oz) gruyère or
emmenthal cheese, grated
½ level teaspoon salt
pinch black pepper or
cayenne*

Additions to the sauce:
*2 hard-boiled eggs, chopped,
or 120 g (4 oz) minced
cooked chicken or turkey or
ham, or 120 g (4 oz) finely
chopped and sautéed
mushrooms*

For the kromeskis:
*12 thin rashers bacon (140 g,
5 oz)
batter mixture (page 61)*

1. Make a white sauce with the butter or margarine, flour, milk and seasoning (page 68). It should be very thick. Stir in the egg yolk and the grated cheese. Do not re-boil. Add the addition selected, and chill in the refrigerator. When cold, shape into balls the size of small marbles (see Egg and Breadcrumb Dressing – white sauce base, page 14). Chill again. Cut the bacon rashers into 3, and stretch lengthwise. Wrap each piece round a ball.

2.  Dip in the batter and deep fry at 200° C (400° F) until light brown.

Suitable for freezing, except for the addition of hard boiled egg (see Deep Freezing, page 15). May be prepared in advance to the end of 1. Continue with 2.

All the recipes in this chapter may be prepared using a flour, egg and breadcrumb dressing (see Pork Meatballs, page 40) instead of batter, and deep fried. They may be frozen, or prepared in advance in the same way.

# 2(g). Sauces and Dips

# *Hot Sauces*

### Barbecue Sauce   Makes 2 dl (⅓ pint)

*45 g (1½ oz) butter*
*60 g (2 oz) onions, finely chopped*
*1 level dessertspoon tomato paste*
*3 tablespoons vinegar*
*1½ level teaspoons demerara sugar*

*2 level teaspoons dry mustard, mixed with a little of the vinegar*
*2 tablespoons Worcestershire sauce*
*1½ dl (¼ pint) water or stock*
*2 rounded teaspoons flour*
*salt and black pepper*

Melt the butter, fry the onions gently for 5 minutes or until soft, add the flour, mix well, add the liquid all at once, take off the heat and stir or whisk till blended and smooth. Add the rest of the ingredients and simmer 10–15 minutes, adjusting the seasoning if necessary. Serve hot.

Suitable for freezing and for preparing in advance.

### Sweet-sour Sauce   Makes 2 dl (⅓ pint)

*20 g (¾ oz) demerara sugar*
*1 tablespoon wine vinegar*
*just under 1 tablespoon soy sauce*
*1 slightly rounded teaspoon cornflour*

*¾ dl (⅛ pint) water*
*¼ green pepper, finely diced*
*60 g (2 oz) pineapple pieces, well crushed*
*salt and pepper*

Warm the sugar, vinegar and soy sauce together, and stir till the sugar has melted. Mix the cornflour in a little of the water, add the rest of the water, and pour the mixture into the pan. Heat, stirring, till thickened. Add the diced green pepper and crushed pineapple, and simmer for 5 minutes. Adjust seasoning, if necessary. Serve hot.

Suitable for freezing and for preparing in advance.

### Pineapple Sauce   Makes 2 dl (⅓ pint)

*45 g (1½ oz) butter or margarine*
*1 teaspoon demerara sugar*
*2 dl (⅓ pint) pineapple juice*

*2 teaspoons lemon juice*
*3 teaspoons cornflour*
*salt and pepper*

Warm the butter and sugar, and stir till the sugar has melted. Mix the cornflour with a little of the pineapple juice, and add the rest of the pineapple and lemon juice, with the cornflour, to the pan. Stir till thickened, and simmer 2–3 minutes. Adjust seasoning and serve hot.

Suitable for freezing and for preparing in advance.

## Chilli Sauce   Makes 2 dl (⅓ pint)

*220 g (7 oz) tin of tomato juice*
*3 large tomatoes, skinned and de-seeded*
*half a red sweet pepper, fresh or tinned, chopped finely*
*3 rounded teaspoons demerara sugar*

*1 tablespoon wine vinegar*
*½ level teaspoon salt*
*¼ level teaspoon black pepper*
*½ level teaspoon cinnamon*
*1 level teaspoon ginger*
*¼ level teaspoon cayenne pepper*

Simmer all the ingredients together with the lid on for 15 minutes. Remove the lid, and reduce till 2 dl (⅓ pint) remains. For a smooth sauce, sieve or pulverize in a blender.

Suitable for freezing or for preparing in advance.

## Fresh Tomato Sauce   Makes 2 dl (⅓ pint)

*450 g (1 lb) tomatoes, roughly chopped (or use tinned tomatoes, drained of all juice)*
*170 g (6 oz) onions, finely chopped*
*3 tablespoons oil or olive oil*

*1 level teaspoon salt*
*1 level teaspoon sugar*
*pinch cayenne pepper*
*½ small clove garlic, crushed*
*1 bayleaf*
*pepper*

Simmer all ingredients together very gently for ½ hour. Sieve, to remove the tomato seeds, skins and the bayleaf. This should leave 2 dl (⅓ pint) but if there is more, return to the pan, and reduce further. Adjust seasoning, if necessary, and serve hot.

Suitable for freezing and for preparing in advance.

## Hollandaise Sauce   Makes 110 g (4 oz)

1½ egg yolks                                   1 teaspoon lemon juice
110 g (4 oz) salted butter

Place the egg yolks in a blender, add the very hot melted butter very slowly while the blender is rotating. When thick add the lemon juice and blend for a few seconds more. Serve at once, or keep warm in a bowl of warm water, but it is very liable to curdle.

ALTERNATIVE METHOD BY HAND
3 egg yolks                                    1 tablespoon white wine
110 g (4 oz) salted butter                     ½ teaspoon lemon juice
4 tablespoons water                            pepper

Place the water, wine, lemon juice and pepper in a small pan, and reduce by boiling to one third of the original amount. Add the egg yolks, one at a time, and stir each in well, preferably with a whisk. Place in a bowl over very hot water, or in a double boiler, adding the butter gradually, in small pieces, until absorbed by the sauce. If it curdles, take off the heat and stir very hard. If it continues to curdle, start again with one more egg yolk, adding a little of the curdled sauce at a time, and beating it until it is incorporated before adding more.

Not suitable for freezing. May be prepared in advance and kept warm in a bowl of warm water, but it is always liable to curdle. Once cold, do not try to re-heat.

## White Sauce   Makes 170 g (6 oz)

20 g (¾ oz) plain flour                        2¼ dl (⅜ pint) milk
20 g (¾ oz) butter or                          salt and pepper
  margarine

Melt the fat in the pan, add the flour, stir well and continue to cook together for 1–2 minutes, but do not let the flour colour. Remove from the heat, add the milk, all at once, and stir, either with a wooden spoon, or a whisk. Return to the heat, and continue to beat until the sauce has become thick and smooth. Simmer for 2–3 minutes. Add seasoning.

Suitable for freezing and for preparing in advance. If leaving for more than a few minutes lay a piece of greaseproof paper or foil on the top of the sauce to prevent a skin forming.

# *Cold Sauces and Dips*

### **Tartare Sauce**      Makes 2 dl (⅓ pint)

*1 hard-boiled egg yolk*
*1 raw egg yolk*
*1½ dl (¼ pint) oil or olive oil*
*1 dessertspoon wine vinegar*
*1 teaspoon capers, finely*
  *chopped*

*1 dessertspoon gherkins,*
  *finely chopped*
*1 teaspoon parsley or other*
  *fresh herbs, finely chopped*
*2 tablespoons thin cream*
*salt and pepper*

All ingredients should first be at room temperature. Sieve the hard-boiled egg yolk, beat in the raw yolk gradually, and then add the oil drop by drop, beating continually, till it has all amalgamated. Add the vinegar and beat again. Stir in the capers, gherkins and herbs, and dilute with the cream if necessary. Season.

Not suitable for freezing. May be prepared in advance and kept cool.


### **Mayonnaise**      Makes 170 g (6 oz)

*2 dl (⅓ pint) oil or olive oil*
*1½ egg yolks*
*1 level teaspoon castor sugar*
*¼ level teaspoon salt*
*¼ level teaspoon white pepper*

*½ level teaspoon dry mustard,*
  *mixed with a few drops of oil*
*2 teaspoons white wine*
  *vinegar*

All ingredients should first be at room temperature. Place the yolks in a bowl, add the salt, pepper and sugar. Beat with a wooden spoon until they thicken slightly, and start to go sticky. Add the mustard and beat again. Add the oil, drop by drop, beating each time until it has been incorporated into the mixture, before adding more. Gradually increase the amount of oil once the sauce is thickening. When it becomes too thick to handle easily, add a little of the vinegar, and continue with the rest of the oil, adding vinegar when necessary. If the mayonnaise should curdle, start again using the remaining half egg yolk, adding a drop of the mixture at a time, and repeat the process as before. The addition of a very little boiling water at the end is often advocated, but although this helps to prevent the sauce curdling later, it thins the sauce, and is not really necessary if all ingredients are at room temperature to begin with.

Not suitable for freezing. May be prepared in advance and kept cool.

VARIATIONS – to make 170 g (6 oz)

SPICY MAYONNAISE
2 rounded tablespoons (110 g,
  4 oz) mayonnaise
1 rounded tablespoon (60 g,
  2 oz) Dijon mustard
4 teaspoons Worcestershire
  sauce
pinch salt
6 tiny pinches cayenne pepper

MUSTARDY MAYONNAISE
1 rounded and 1 level
  tablespoon (90 g, 3 oz)
  mayonnaise
1 rounded and 1 level
  tablespoon (90 g, 3 oz) Dijon
  mustard
1½ teaspoon icing sugar, or
  ground castor sugar

CURRY MAYONNAISE
2 rounded tablespoons (110 g,
  4 oz) mayonnaise
4 rounded teaspoons apple or
  other chutney
2 rounded teaspoons curry
  powder

HORSERADISH MAYONNAISE
1 rounded and 1 level
  tablespoon (90 g, 3 oz)
  mayonnaise
1 rounded and 1 level
  tablespoon (90 g, 3 oz)
  tableready horseradish sauce
pinch salt

GREEN MAYONNAISE (SAUCE VERTE)
3 slightly rounded
  tablespoons (150 g, 5½ oz)
  mayonnaise
1 tablespoon thick cream
  (30 g, 1 oz)

2–3 sprays parsley
2–3 leaves spinach
a few chives or other fresh
  green herbs

Simmer the herbs and spinach in a very little, very slightly salted
water for 5–10 minutes. Remove from the water and dry, then sieve
into the mayonnaise and cream mixture.

CHILLI MAYONNAISE
1 rounded and 1 level
  tablespoon (90 g, 3 oz)
  mayonnaise
3 tablespoons (90 g, 3 oz)
  Chilli Sauce (page 67)
½ teaspoon onion, finely
  grated, or onion juice,
  optional
1 teaspoon Worcestershire
  sauce, optional
1½ teaspoons lemon juice,
  optional

PAPRIKA MAYONNAISE
2 rounded tablespoons (110 g,
  4 oz) mayonnaise
1 level teaspoon paprika
1 rounded tablespoon (60 g,
  2 oz) tomato ketchup

AIOLI (GARLIC MAYONNAISE)

10 tablespoons olive oil
2–3 cloves garlic, crushed
2 egg yolks

few drops lemon juice
salt and white pepper
cream if necessary

Crush the garlic cloves with the egg yolks. Add the olive oil drop by drop, as in the making of Mayonnaise (page 69) diluting with lemon juice when necessary. This makes a very thick sauce, but if being used as a dip, should be diluted with thin cream. Add salt and pepper to taste.

### Vinaigrette    Makes 2 dl (⅓ pint)

6 tablespoons oil or olive oil
1 tablespoon wine vinegar
1 rounded teaspoon sugar, if wished

½ level teaspoon salt
black pepper

Mix all ingredients together, preferably in a screw-top jar. The oil is liable to separate from the other ingredients, and the jar should be shaken vigorously just before use.

May be prepared in advance, and kept cool.

### Avocado Dip    Makes 170 g (6 oz)

110 g (4 oz) avocado pulp
2 teaspoons lemon juice
¼ clove garlic, crushed
10 g (⅓ oz) onion, finely chopped

30 g (1 oz) soft cream cheese
1½ tablespoons oil or olive oil
1 tablespoon milk

Mix all ingredients together, and blend, preferably in an electric machine, until smooth.

Not suitable for freezing. May be prepared in advance and kept cool. The lemon juice will prevent the avocado turning black.

### Avocado and Tunafish Dip    Makes 170 g (6 oz)

90 g (3 oz) avocado pulp
2 teaspoons lemon juice
10 g (⅓ oz) onion, chopped
30 g (1 oz) soft cream cheese

1½ tablespoons oil or olive oil
30 g (1 oz) tunafish, plus a little of its oil
2 teaspoons milk

Mix all ingredients together and blend, preferably in an electric machine, until smooth.

Not suitable for freezing. May be prepared in advance and kept cool.

## Crab and Avocado Dip
Makes 170 g
(6 oz)

*90 g (3 oz) tinned or fresh crab*      *90 g (3 oz) ready-made*
                                        *Avocado Dip (page 71)*

Mix the ingredients together, and blend, preferably in an electric
machine until smooth. Dilute, if necessary, with juice from the tin, or
thin cream.

Not suitable for freezing. May be prepared in advance and kept cool.


## Seafood Dip
Makes 170 g (6 oz)

*6 tablespoons (140 g, 5 oz)*           *2 level teaspoons chopped*
  *tomato ketchup*                        *onion, or onion juice*
*4 teaspoons wine vinegar*              *few drops Worcestershire*
*2–4 drops tabasco sauce*                 *sauce*
*2 level teaspoons horseradish*         *pinch salt*
  *sauce*

Mix all ingredients together until well blended.

Suitable for freezing, and may be prepared in advance and kept
chilled.


## Basic Creamy Dip
Makes 170 g
(6 oz)

*90 g (3 oz) soft cream cheese*         *2–3 teaspoons thin cream*
*1 rounded and 1 level*                 *salt and pepper*
  *tablespoon (90 g 3 oz)*
  *Mayonnaise (page 69)*

Blend the soft cream cheese and mayonnaise together, and dilute
with the cream. Season.

Not suitable for freezing. May be prepared in advance and kept cool.


## Smoked Salmon Dip
Makes 170 g
(6 oz)

*60 g (2 oz) smoked salmon,*            *15 g (½ oz) onion, finely*
  *either from a jar, or buy*             *chopped*
  *'scraps' from a delicatessen*        *2½ tablespoons oil*
*20 g (¾ oz) white crustless*           *2½ tablespoons cream*
  *bread, soaked in a little milk,*     *1 teaspoon lemon juice*
  *and squeezed out*

Mix all ingredients together, and blend, preferably in an electric machine, until smooth.

Not suitable for freezing. May be prepared in advance and kept cool.

### Tunafish Dip  Makes 170 g (6 oz)

*120 g (4½ oz) tunafish,*
  *including some oil*
*10 g (⅓ oz) crustless white*
  *bread, soaked in a little milk,*
  *and squeezed out*

*1 tablespoon oil*
*1 teaspoon lemon juice*
*1 tablespoon thin cream*
*salt and pepper*

Mix all ingredients together, and blend, preferably in an electric machine until smooth.

Suitable for freezing, and may be prepared in advance and kept cool.

### Taramasalata  Makes 170 g (6 oz)

*60 g (2 oz) smoked cod's roe*
*2 tablespoons thin cream*
*15 g (½ oz) white crustless*
  *bread, soaked in a little milk*
  *and squeezed out*

*20 g (¾ oz) onion, finely*
  *chopped*
*2 tablespoons olive oil*
*½ tablespoon lemon juice*

Soak the cod's roe in a little milk for 1–2 hours, if very dry. Remove any skin, and mix all ingredients together; blend, preferably in an electric machine, till smooth.

Suitable for freezing, and may be prepared in advance and kept refrigerated for 2–3 days.

### Clam Dip  Makes 170 g (6 oz)

This recipe comes from Mrs Claire Glovin of Sudbury, Mass.

*45 g (1½ oz) tinned clams*
*90 g (3 oz) soft cream cheese*
*10 g (⅓ oz) onion, chopped*
*1 dash Worcestershire sauce*

*½ teaspoon lemon juice*
*1 tablespoon clam juice*
*pepper*

Place all ingredients in an electric machine, and blend till smooth. Add more of the juice from the clams if necessary. There is no need to add salt.

Not suitable for freezing. May be prepared in advance and kept cool.

## Prawn and Pine Nuts Dip    Makes 170 g
(6 oz)

1 small onion, grated very
 finely
60 g (2 oz) prawns, shelled and
 finely chopped

15 g (½ oz) pine kernels
2 rounded tablespoons (120 g,
 4 oz) mayonnaise

Mix the ingredients together.

Not suitable for freezing. May be prepared in advance and kept cool.

## Chick-peas Dip    Makes 170 g (6 oz)

150 g (5 oz) chick-peas, tinned
1 teaspoon lemon juice
7 teaspoons olive oil

4 teaspoons juice from the tin
salt and pepper
1 small clove garlic, crushed

Mix all ingredients together, and blend, preferably in an electric
machine, till smooth.

Suitable for freezing. May be prepared in advance and kept cool.

## Prawn and Cream Cheese Dip    Makes 170 g
(6 oz)

60 g (2 oz) soft cream cheese
60 g (2 oz) prawns, finely
 chopped
2 tablespoons thin cream

1 teaspoon tomato paste
2–3 pinches paprika
salt and pepper

Mix the cream cheese with the cream, add the tomato paste and
paprika, and finally the chopped prawns. Season.

Not suitable for freezing. May be prepared in advance and kept cool.

## Blue Cheese Dip    Makes 170 g (6 oz)

90 g (3 oz) soft cream cheese
40 g (1⅓ oz) blue cheese

3–4 tablespoons milk or thin
 cream
4 drops lemon juice

Blend the two cheeses with the milk or cream, varying the amounts
of each cheese according to their strength. The amount of milk or
cream required will vary according to the dryness of the blue cheese.
Stir in the lemon juice.

Not suitable for freezing. May be prepared in advance and kept cool.

### Garlic Dip          Makes 170 g (6 oz)

*140 g (5 oz) soft cream cheese     1 clove garlic, crushed*
*3 tablespoons milk*

Blend the cream cheese with the milk, and mix in the garlic.

Not suitable for freezing. May be prepared in advance and kept cool.

### Bacon Dip          Makes 170 g (6 oz)

*120 g (4 oz) soft cream cheese     120 g (4 oz) bacon*
*3 tablespoons milk or thin*
  *cream*

Grill the bacon till crisp. Cool, and crumble. Blend the cream cheese with the milk or cream, and add the bacon.

Not suitable for freezing. May be prepared in advance and kept cool.

### Cream Cheese and Stuffed Olive Dip          Makes
170 g (6 oz)

*120 g (4 oz) soft cream cheese     15 stuffed olives, finely*
*3 tablespoons milk or thin          chopped*
  *cream*

Blend the cream cheese with the milk or cream, and add the olives.

Not suitable for freezing. May be prepared in advance and kept cool.

### Sour Cream and Beetroot Dip          Makes
170 g (6 oz)

*3 tablespoons (90 g, 3 oz) sour     90 g (3 oz) beetroot, in sweet*
  *cream                               vinegar*

Drain the beetroot, mash, and add to the sour cream. Season if necessary.

Not suitable for freezing. May be prepared in advance and kept cool.

### Serving Suggestions

Serve in china or glass bowls, surrounded by Crudités (page 32), crisps, savoury biscuits, Baby Kebabs (page 49) or prawns, etc., on sticks.

They can also be served in bowls made from a red or green cabbage, cut in half, and hollowed out; or from a pineapple from which the top has been removed, and the inside hollowed out; or from half a melon, hollowed out.

In each case make sure the base is flat enough to support it securely, or slice a piece off, to make it flat.

# 3

# CANAPÉS
# AND SANDWICHES

## 3(a). Cold Canapés and Sandwiches

**EACH RECIPE MAKES 36**

## *Cold Canapés*

### Method and Deep Freezing

Cold canapés differ from open sandwiches in that the open sandwiches are made for the most part from simple ingredients, such as
slices of ham, beef, etc., prawns, shrimps, smoked salmon, etc., and
garnishes of parsley, chives, chopped onion, etc. Cold canapés are

made from made-up recipes such as those that follow. They should be placed on small pieces of very firm bread, or crispbread, or toast, or bread fried in shallow oil and allowed to cool. They can be round, square or triangular.

Canapés can usually be prepared a few hours in advance, as long as the bases have been well buttered to prevent drying out, or going soggy. It is inadvisable to prepare canapés on a crispbread base more than a short time ahead. Those on crisp fried bread will stay crisp for three or four hours, and the bases themselves can be made the day before, and kept in an airtight tin.

Most of the canapés are suitable for freezing. They must be frozen first on open trays, and when firm, packed carefully into containers. To thaw, replace the canapés on trays while still frozen, or on the plates from which they are to be served, allowing 30 minutes for thawing. Only those containing egg in any form, soft cream cheese, mayonnaise or salads, such as tomatoes, cucumber, lettuce, etc., should not be frozen.

### Salami Canapés

*90 g (3 oz) salami, chopped
.very finely
60 g (2 oz) red sweet peppers,
chopped
60 g (2 oz) green sweet
peppers, chopped*

*3 teaspoons onion, finely
chopped
45 g (1½ oz) soft cream cheese
1 level tablespoon Mayonnaise
(page 69)
salt and black pepper*

Blend the mayonnaise and the cream cheese together, and add all the other ingredients. Spread over the bases.

### Olive, Ham and Green Pepper Canapés

*75 g (2½ oz) stuffed olives,
finely chopped
45 g (1½ oz) green sweet
peppers, finely chopped
45 g (1½ oz) ham, finely
chopped*

*45 g (1½ oz) soft cream cheese
1 slightly rounded tablespoon
Mayonnaise (page 69)
salt and black pepper*

Blend the mayonnaise and cream cheese together, and add all the other ingredients. Spread over the bases.

## Anchovy and Walnut Canapés

*4 anchovies in oil, minced or
   chopped
2 tablespoons oil, from the tin
   or add extra oil
60 g (2 oz) chopped walnuts*

*1 teaspoon lemon juice
2 teaspoons parsley, chopped
¼ clove garlic, crushed
75 g (2½ oz) soft cream cheese
salt and black pepper*

Mash the cream cheese and gradually add the oil, lemon juice and the other ingredients, except the parsley. Spread over the bases. Garnish with the parsley.

## Scotch Woodcock

*Scrambled Egg (page 111)
   using 40 g (1½ oz) butter or
   margarine and 4 large eggs*

*anchovies*

See page 105, but spread the scrambled egg onto the bases only when cold. Garnish with anchovies.

## Hard-boiled Egg and Caviare Canapés

*75 g (2½ oz) (1 jar) red
   lumpfish caviare
6 teaspoons chopped onion
½ teaspoon lemon juice*

*1½ hard-boiled eggs
1 tablespoon Mayonnaise
   (page 69)
salt and black pepper*

Dice the hard-boiled eggs, or chop very finely indeed, and mix carefully with the mayonnaise. It may be necessary to use a little more, depending on the consistency of the mayonnaise. Mix the caviare, the onion and the lemon juice together. Spread the egg mayonnaise in a circle round the edge of the canapé, and fill the middle with the caviare mixture. Alternatively, place the egg mayonnaise in the middle and the caviare round the outside.

## Hard-boiled Egg and Bacon Canapés

*60 g (2 oz) bacon, minced or
   chopped finely
2 hard-boiled eggs, finely
   chopped*

*4 tablespoons Mayonnaise
   (page 69)
1 tablespoon oil
salt and black pepper*

Fry the bacon in the oil, till crisp. Cool, and crumble. Add to the hard-boiled eggs, and mix into the mayonnaise. Spread over the bases.

## Salmon Canapés

90 g (3 oz) cold boiled salmon,
    flaked
2 hard-boiled eggs, chopped
    finely

20 stuffed olives, chopped
    finely
4 tablespoons Mayonnaise
    (page 69)
salt and black pepper

Mix all ingredients together, and spread over the bases.

## Crab Mayonnaise Canapés

125 g (4½ oz) crabmeat, flaked
2 teaspoons lemon juice
5 tablespoons of any of the
    following, mixed in any
    proportion: parsley, finely
    chopped onion, chives,
    celery, green or red sweet
    peppers

2½ tablespoons thick
    Mayonnaise (page 69)
salt and black pepper

Mix all ingredients together, and spread over the bases.

## Devilled Crab Canapés

Ingredients and method as in Crab Mayonnaise Canapés (above),
adding:

1 slightly rounded teaspoon
    curry powder
1 teaspoon tomato paste
1 level teaspoon Dijon
    mustard

4 dashes Worcestershire
    sauce
2 pinches cayenne pepper

## Shrimps in Butter

185 g (6½ oz) shrimps
110 g (4 oz) butter

1 teaspoon lemon juice
pinch cayenne

Simmer the shrimps in the butter, and add the lemon juice and
cayenne. Cool, and spread over the bases.

## Bread Pinwheels

7 large slices of fresh white or
    brown bread, at least 14 cm
    (5½ in) in one direction

60 g (2 oz) softened butter
various fillings, see below

Chill the bread in the refrigerator, and remove the crusts. Lay the slices between two dampened tea towels and roll with a rolling pin to flatten slightly. This makes it easier to deal with. Butter to the edges, cover with filling and roll up tightly up the 14 cm (5½ in) length. Wrap lightly in foil, screw up the ends to hold it firm, and refrigerate. Remove the foil and cut into thin slices, approximately 1 cm (⅓ in) wide.

FILLINGS FOR PINWHEELS
A. Smoked salmon or Swedish marinated salmon (gravlax). The weight varies with the thickness, but using thin slices requires 110 g (4 oz). Add a squeeze of lemon juice.
B. Tunafish Pâté (page 95), Taramasalata (page 73), Chicken Liver Pâté, (page 93), Smoked Salmon Pâté (page 94) etc., 170 g (6 oz).
C. Ham and asparagus, laying the ham on the bread, and the asparagus near the end you are rolling from. These may need to be secured with a cocktail stick. Using very thin ham, 140 g (5 oz). Spreading a little soft cream cheese on the ham helps it to remain rolled.
D. Ham, chicken or turkey, minced, and soft cream cheese, mixing the cheese with a little milk. 110 g (4 oz) soft cream cheese, with 10 teaspoons milk, and 140 g (5 oz) meat.

## Beef, Pork or Smoked Reindeer Pinwheels

*36 bases of pumpernickel or*     *140 g (5 oz) Horseradish*
  *brown bread*                         *Spread (page 95)*
*5 slices of meat,*
  *approximately 15 cm by 9 cm*
  *(5 in by 3½ in)*

Spread the Horseradish Spread over the slices of meat. (Add a little lemon juice, Worcestershire sauce, and tabasco as a variation.) Roll from the narrow end up the longer length, very firmly. Refrigerate, in foil, until very cold. Using a very sharp knife cut into slices 1 cm (⅓ in) wide, tidying away the untidy ends. Place on rounds of pumpernickel or firm brown bread. Garnish the pork with tiny sections of pineapple or peach, and secure them with a cocktail stick. The beef and smoked reindeer need no garnish. The colour contrast with the white filling is enough. It is possible sometimes to use the untidy ends by inserting a small piece of pineapple, stuffed olive, etc., in the middle, where there tends to be a hole.

## Tunnel Rolls

7 large slices of white or
  brown bread

140 g (5 oz) pâté (pages 92–5)
60 g (2 oz) softened butter

Prepare the bread as in the recipe for Pinwheels (page 80). Butter the bread. Lay a sausage shape of pâté near the near end of the bread, allowing approximately 20 g (just under 1 oz) per slice of bread. Roll the bread over so that the two edges just meet. Cut away any excess bread and use as buttered bases. Roll tightly in foil, twisting the ends, place a cocktail stick through to secure, and refrigerate till very cold. Cut in straight or diagonal slices, tidying away the untidy ends, making 5 rolls per slice. Serve on cocktail sticks.

## Beef, Pork or Smoked Reindeer Tunnels

36 pumpernickel or bread
  bases
9 slices of meat,
  approximately 13 cm by 7 cm
  (5 in by 2¾ in), weighing
  20–25 g (just under 1 oz
  each)

225 g (8 oz) Horseradish
  Spread (page 95)

Place 30 g (1 oz) of the spread in a sausage shape across the wider width of the meat, about 2½ cm (1 in) from the near end. Cover with the near end of the meat and roll to the other, so that the ends of the meat just overlap. Roll lightly in foil and refrigerate until very cold. Cut each roll into 4, cutting away the untidy ends. It is more economical to cut straight across, but looks nice cut diagonally. Place on pumpernickel or firm brown bread bases.

## Baby 'English' Sandwiches

These are very tiny sandwiches, made from two or more layers of bread or pumpernickel, sometimes using different pâtés or spreads in the same sandwich.

Allow 110 g (4 oz) softened butter to make 36 sandwiches, or mix the butter with a little Mayonnaise (page 69).

First slice the bread, then do all the spreading, then the filling and finally the cutting. This requires more space, but saves time.

## Striped Sandwiches

16 slices of mixed brown and
  white fresh bread, cut very
  thinly

savoury butters (page 86–7),
  pâtés or spreads (pages
  92–7)
110 g (4 oz) butter

Butter the slices of bread, and spread all but two with a variety of savoury butters, pâtés or spreads, which will blend together in flavour, but contrast in colour. Place the 14 slices on top of each other in two piles, 7 slices in a pile. Place the last two slices on top buttered side down. Wrap tightly in foil and refrigerate, preferably overnight, with a weight on top of each. Remove the foil, and slice down through the layers, as though slicing a loaf. Cut the slices into squares, trianges, etc.

# 3(b). Open Sandwiches

**EACH RECIPE MAKES 36 SANDWICHES**

## Method and Ingredients

Open sandwiches consist of a base, such as rye bread, spread with either butter or a simple spread, one or two main ingredients such as shrimps and mayonnaise, and a garnish, such as chopped parsley. They should be very small, approximately 3 cm (1¼ in) square.

THE BASE
This should be firm. It can be made from savoury biscuits, crispbread cut to a suitable size, or from several varieties of bread. Suitable varieties of bread include pumpernickel, German volkornbrot, German 'black' bread, rye bread, small rounds of fresh French bread, etc. It should be about ½ cm (¼ in) thick, unless very close-textured, in which case it can be thinner. They can be prepared some hours in advance, except in the case of biscuits or crispbread, which tend to go soggy. The bread is more easily cut if chilled in the refrigerator before cutting. They can be cut in a variety of shapes, round, square, rectangular, triangular and in diamonds.

BUTTERS AND SPREADS
Always butter to the very edge of the base. This helps to keep the bread fresh and to prevent it curling up if left for any time. It also acts

as a waterproof layer between the base and the ingredient, to prevent the bread becoming too soggy. Be generous with the butter – not only will the sandwich taste better, but a generous amount helps to make the ingredient stick. You don't want everything to fall off when the sandwich is tilted. Flavoured butters and spreads add extra flavour to the sandwich.

### MAIN INGREDIENTS

Use only one ingredient with a strong flavour, and if you want to use two ingredients make sure they blend well and do not conflict. Smoked salmon and cold scrambled egg go well together; smoked salmon and anchovies don't.

Make sure you have no hidden dangers; don't use a whole slice of cucumber hidden under a mass of mayonnaise, which will come out unexpectedly when your guest takes a small bite. Make everything small enough for easy eating. Make it quite clear what's inside. Some people may not be able to eat certain foods, or they may not like them. Don't disguise the main ingredients by a mass of garnish.

### GARNISHES

These are either to decorate the sandwich to improve its appearance by providing a contrast in colour, or to complement the flavour. They should be used very discreetly, and should never be so generous as to disguise the original flavour, or so large as to make the sandwich difficult to eat. Chopped parsley, the simplest of all garnishes, is often the best.

### DOUBLE SANDWICHES

This is another way of making an open sandwich. Use very firm bread, and cut each piece approximately 6½ cm by 3 cm (2½ in by 1¼ in) long. Use two contrasting fillings, placing one on each half, like a domino, for example, cold scrambled egg and smoked salmon, or marinated herring and egg mayonnaise, or black caviare and a cream cheese spread. Garnish in the usual way.

### TIME-SAVING

Use mass-production methods to make them, if you have the room. It is a very long process making one sandwich after the other, but if you can lay out all the bread, then do all the buttering, all the laying on of main ingredients, and all the garnishing at once, it cuts down the time required enormously.

Another time-saving method is to chill an unsliced loaf in the refrigerator. When very cold remove crusts down the sides and ends, and slice horizontally. Firm brown bread is the best for this. Cut each long slice lengthwise into two long strips. Butter and decorate each strip, piping down the edges and filling in the middle, for example with cream cheese and garlic spread, slightly softened with a little extra cream, and black or red caviare in the middle. Cut into small sandwiches either by cutting straight across to make rectangles, or diagonally to make triangles.

FINALLY
Offer a selection of sandwiches on the same plate, never all of one kind, which looks dull and unappetising. Think about the colours as well as the flavours.

If making them in advance, cover with a damp cloth, or foil, and keep in an airtight container, or a cool place. Otherwise they will dry out, and the decoration will go limp. It is far better to prepare all the ingredients well in advance – hard-boil and shell the eggs, slice the radishes, prepare the savoury butters, etc., and then assemble everything at the last moment. Do remember to take the butter out of the refrigerator in good time – there is nothing more annoying than to have everything ready and find the butter is hard. Softening in the oven or over hot water is a possibility, but very often it turns to oil while your back is turned.

## Deep Freezing of Open Sandwiches

Most sandwiches are suitable for freezing. They should be frozen uncovered on a flat tray, and when firm packed carefully into containers. Anything likely to become dislodged should be secured with cocktail sticks, though this uses a lot of space. Thaw by placing again on trays, or directly onto the plates from which they will be served, for 30 minutes.

Sandwiches containing any form of egg, soft cream cheese, mayonnaise or salads are not suitable for freezing.

## Savoury Butters

HORSERADISH BUTTER
*45 g (1½ oz) tableready*
  *horseradish sauce, mixed*
  *with*
*45 g (1½ oz) butter*

ANCHOVY BUTTER
*12 anchovy fillets in oil and*
*½ clove garlic (optional)*
  *crushed, mixed with*
*60 g (2 oz) butter*

WATERCRESS BUTTER
*2 teaspoons watercress, finely*
  *chopped*
*1 teaspoon parsley, finely*
  *chopped, mixed with*
  *60 g (2 oz) butter*

MAYONNAISE BUTTER
*1 tablespoon Mayonnaise*
  *(page 69), mixed with*
*45 g (1½ oz) butter*

PIMENTO BUTTER
⅔ of a large red sweet pepper,
 tinned, bottled (not in
 vinegar) or fresh with skin
 removed by blanching, and a
few drops lemon juice, mixed
 with
60 g (2 oz) butter

LOBSTER BUTTER
45 g (1½ oz) lobster or crab or
 prawns, well mashed
½ teaspoon lemon juice,
 mixed with
60 g (2 oz) butter

CURRY BUTTER
1 teaspoon and 1 level
 teaspoon chutney
1 slightly rounded teaspoon
 curry powder
1 level teaspoon made English
 mustard
few drops lemon juice
salt and pinch cayenne
dash Worcestershire sauce,
 mixed with
45 g (1½ oz) butter

## Spreads

Use any of the pâtés or spreads on pages 92–7, on top of butter, and add only a very simple main ingredient, such as sliced gherkins, radishes or olives, etc.

## Main Ingredients

*Prawns*: using 1 or 2 per sandwich, you require 225 g (8 oz) already shelled, 450 g (1 lb) with shells
*Smoked salmon, Swedish marinated salmon (gravlax)*: 90 g (3 oz)
*Smoked eel*: 90 g (3 oz) if using in conjunction with scrambled egg; 170 g (6 oz) if alone
*Smoked trout, kipper or herring*: 150 g (5½ oz)
*Anchovies*: 2 tins, 60 g (2 oz)
*Sardines*: 1 tin, 125 g (4½ oz)
*Red or black lumpfish caviare*: 2 jars at 75 g (2½ oz) each if used alone. 75 g (2½ oz) if used as garnish with egg mayonnaise, etc.
*Salami*: 60 g (2 oz) cut into thin slices and divided
*Hard-boiled egg*: 3 eggs, cutting each into 6 slices, and cutting each slice in half
*Beef, pork or smoked reindeer*: 110 g (4 oz) cut in very thin slices, and divided

*Marinated kippers*:
 1 filleted kipper
 2 teaspoons lemon juice
 slice onion
 3 teaspoons oil
 salt and pepper

Pour the lemon juice and oil over the kipper and add the onion and pinches of seasoning. Leave overnight. Slice diagonally like a miniature smoked salmon.

*Potato salad*:
110 g (4 oz) boiled, cold potatoes, cut into very tiny cubes
45 g (1½ oz) Mayonnaise (page 69)
1 teaspoon chopped onion
chopped chives or parsley to garnish

Mix the chopped potatoes with the onions and mayonnaise. Garnish with the chives or parsley.

*Beetroot salad*:
110 g (4 oz) boiled beetroot, skinned and chopped into very tiny cubes
30 g (1 oz) Mayonnaise (page 69)
½ teaspoon chopped onion
chopped white of 2 hard-boiled eggs to garnish

Mix the chopped beetroot with the mayonnaise and onion. Garnish with the chopped hard-boiled egg.

## Garnishes

*Mushrooms*: 30 g (1 oz), raw, cut into very thin slices
*Radishes or celery*: finely chopped or sliced
*Asparagus tips*
*Onion or leek rings*, raw, cut very thin, or chopped finely
*Red or green sweet peppers*, cut very thin
*Tomato slices*: 2 average tomatoes cut into 36 tiny pieces
*Mandarin orange sections*
*Lemon slices*, cut very thin
*Nuts*, plain or toasted
*Grapes*, halved and de-seeded: 110 g (4 oz)
*Pineapple*, very small sections
*Tinned peaches*, very small sections
*Apples*, cut into thin slivers
*Banana*: 1 large, cut into 36 very thin slices
*Dill*, in very small sprigs
*Fresh herbs*, in very small sprigs or leaves, or chopped
*Celery leaves*, only young and green
*Cocktail onions*
*Stuffed or black olives*, sliced: 45 g (1½ oz)
*Chopped aspic jelly* (page 89)
*Mustard or sweet pickle*
*Capers*

*Gherkins*, sliced
*Red or black lumpfish caviare*
*Small shrimps*
*Smoked salmon*, tiny piece round an asparagus tip
*Anchovies*, finely sliced
*Frankfurter sausage*, finely sliced
*Bacon*, cooked and crumbled: 75 g (2½ oz) thin rashers
*Hard-boiled egg*, sliced or chopped
*Scrambled egg* (page 105), using 4 eggs
*Piped rosettes of horseradish cream*, or other savoury creams
*Piped rosettes of smoked salmon cream, etc.*, in tubes from a
    delicatessen
*Gruyère or other hard cheeses*: 90 g (3 oz) cut into thin slivers

## Aspic Jelly

*3 dl (10 fluid oz) aspic jelly,*
 *made according to the*
 *maker's instructions*

Prepare the open sandwiches on large pieces of bread, covering the bases well with butter to prevent the aspic soaking in. Never use biscuits or crispbread, as these will always go soggy. Leave the crust on the bread, if there is one. Pour the cool, but unset, aspic carefully over the sandwiches, allowing only just enough to form a thin layer of jelly. Mop up any that spills before it can soak into the bread. Refrigerate at once till set, and repeat, making a second layer. Refrigerate again, and when cold cut off the crusts and divide the bread into small sections. Any excess jelly can be refrigerated till set, and cut into tiny cubes to use as decoration.

## 30 Open Sandwiches

|    | *Base* | *Main Ingredient* | *Garnish* |
|----|--------|-------------------|-----------|
| 1. | Butter | Red or black caviare | Very fine onion rings |
| 2. | Butter | Potato Salad (page 88) with a little red or black caviare | Chopped chives |
| 3. | Anchovy Butter (page 86) | Cold scrambled egg (page 111) | Chopped parsley |
| 4. | Watercress Butter (page 86) | Egg Mayonnaise (page 69) with sliced radishes | Chopped chives |

| 5. | Curry Butter (page 87) | Cold shrimps or prawns | Small piece of pineapple |
| 6. | Pimento Butter (page 87) | Crab and small piece of lettuce or watercress | Sliver of lemon |
| 7. | Butter | Chopped prawns, apple and celery in Paprika Mayonnaise (page 70) | Paprika |
| 8. | Mayonnaise Butter (page 86) | Prawn, crab, or lobster with a small piece of sliced cucumber | Chopped chives |
| 9. | Lobster Butter (page 87) | Quartered slices of cucumber overlapping | Piping of Mayonnaise (page 69) |
| 10. | Butter | Chicken Liver Pâté (page 93) | Capers, or slices of celery, or slice of stuffed olive |
| 11. | Butter | Kipper Pâté (page 94) | Half a walnut |
| 12. | Butter | Taramasalata (page 95) | Slices of black olives |
| 13. | Butter | Smoked Buckling Pâté (page 94) | Slices of stuffed olive |
| 14. | Butter | Herb Cheese (page 97) | Sliced radishes |
| 15. | Cream Cheese and Watercress Spread (page 96) | Potted shrimps | Slice of lemon and cayenne |
| 16. | Butter | Fresh salmon and Mayonnaise (page 69) | Sliver of lemon |
| 17. | Butter | Smoked salmon rolled round an asparagus tip | Squeeze lemon juice and chopped parsley |
| 18. | Butter | Cold scrambled egg (page 111) with filleted smoked eel | Squeeze lemon juice and chopped dill |
| 19. | Horseradish Spread (page 95) | Smoked mackerel, trout, buckling, or raw marinated kipper (page 87) | Squeeze lemon juice and sliver of tomato, or sliver of lemon |

| 20. | Butter | Watercress leaves, with piped Smoked Salmon Pâté (page 94) | Sliver of lemon |
|---|---|---|---|
| 21. | Cream Cheese and Garlic Spread (page 96) | Mussels in oil, or a smoked mussel, or a smoked oyster | Squeeze lemon juice and chopped parsley |
| 22. | Butter | Halved meatball, cut side down, with sweet pickle | Chopped red sweet peppers |
| 23. | Butter | Pork and Game Pâté (page 92) | Thin slices of apple or gherkin |
| 24. | Butter | Thin slices of pork with apple sauce | Chopped parsley |
| 25. | Butter | Avocado Spread (page 93) | Half a walnut, or chopped walnuts, or slices of celery |
| 26. | Horseradish Spread (page 95) | Thin slice of rare beef and Beetroot Salad (page 88) | Chopped onion, or a cocktail onion |
| 27. | Cream cheese | Slice of blue cheese | Sliced radishes, or chopped walnut, or halved grapes |
| 28. | Butter | Slice of hard cheese, such as gouda, cheddar, etc., or camembert | Sliced radishes, slices of red or green sweet peppers, or grapes |
| 29. | Mayonnaise Butter (page 86) | Piece of cold duckling | Segment of mandarin orange and chopped parsley |
| 30. | Butter | Cold chicken on a lettuce leaf with Curry Mayonnaise (page 70) | Halved green grapes |

# 3(c). Pâtés and Spreads

## Pork and Game Pâté  Makes 450 g (1 lb)

225 g (8 oz) fat pork
110 g (4 oz) cooked rabbit, hare, duck or any form of game
30 g (1 oz) fat bacon
4 tablespoons dry vermouth
1 tablespoon brandy
6 juniper berries, crushed (optional)
½ clove garlic, crushed

just under 1 level teaspoon salt
black pepper
½ egg, lightly beaten
30 g (1 oz) crustless bread, squeezed out in water or stock
15 g (½ oz) butter or margarine (for the terrine)
3 dl (½ pint) aspic jelly solution (optional)

Chop the cold game roughly. Blend the pork, bacon, garlic, egg and seasonings together till smooth, preferably in an electric blender, or mince very finely together. Marinade the mixture in the vermouth and brandy for at least 2 hours. Add the game, bread and crushed juniper berries, and mix well. Butter a terrine and fill with the mixture. Cover, and place in a bain-marie (a larger dish in which there is enough hot water to come half-way up the side of the terrine), and bake at 130° C (250° F) for 1 hour 15 minutes. Top up the water when necessary. Allow to cool. When cool pour over the aspic jelly solution, made according to the maker's instructions. This is not essential, but it helps to keep the pâté moist. Serve on savoury biscuits, fingers of toast, etc.

Suitable for freezing. Allow 3 hours to thaw. May be prepared in advance, and kept in a refrigerator for up to two weeks.

### Chicken Liver Pâté   Makes 450 g (1 lb)

*450 g (1 lb) chicken livers*          *½ clove garlic, crushed*
*60 g (2 oz) butter*                    *1 level teaspoon salt*
*1 tablespoon brandy*                   *black pepper*
*1 tablespoon medium sherry*

Remove any greenish-coloured bits in the chicken livers. Cook in the butter for 5 minutes. Add the brandy, flame, and allow to bubble 2–3 minutes. Add the sherry, and bubble again. Add the garlic, salt and pepper. Blend together, preferably in an electric blender, till smooth, adding more hot liquid butter if necessary. The pâté should be slightly pink inside.

Suitable for freezing, and for preparing up to a few days in advance and refrigerating.

### German Liver Pâté   Makes 450 g (1 lb)

*335 g (12 oz) kalbsleberwurst*         *¼ clove garlic, crushed*
  *(calf's liver sausage)*              *2 tablespoons brandy*
*75 g (2½ oz) melted butter*            *salt and pepper*

Cook the garlic very gently in the butter for 1 minute, and then add to the liver sausage. Stir in the brandy, salt and pepper. This must be stored in a refrigerator for 2 weeks before eating.

Suitable for freezing, and for preparing in advance and storing in the refrigerator.

### Avocado Spread   Makes 450 g (1 lb)

*300 g (10½ oz) avocado pulp*           *30 g (1 oz) onion, chopped*
*6 teaspoons lemon juice*               *4½ tablespoons oil or olive oil*
*½ clove garlic, crushed*               *salt and pepper*

Blend all ingredients together, preferably in an electric blender, until very smooth.

Not suitable for freezing. May be prepared in advance and kept in a refrigerator for 24 hours.

### Smoked Salmon Pâté Makes 450 g (1 lb)

*170 g (6 oz) jar smoked
    salmon, or 'scraps' from a
    delicatessen
60 g (2 oz) fresh white bread,
    in water or milk, squeezed
    out*

*45 g (1½ oz) onion, finely
    chopped
6 tablespoons oil
6 tablespoons thin cream
1½ teaspoons lemon juice*

Blend all ingredients together, preferably in an electric blender, until very smooth.

Suitable for freezing. May be prepared in advance, and kept refrigerated for 2–3 days.

### Smoked Buckling Pâté    Makes 450 g (1 lb)

*335 g (12 oz) buckling (or
    other smoked fish) after
    filleting and removing skin,
    or 450 g (16 oz) whole
3 teaspoons (30 g, 1 oz) onion,
    finely chopped*

*6 teaspoons lemon juice
6 teaspoons thin cream
6 teaspoons olive oil
salt, depending on the
    saltiness of the fish and
    black pepper*

Blend all ingredients together, preferably in an electric blender; or flake the fish, mix in the other ingredients, and serve unblended.

Not suitable for freezing. May be prepared in advance and kept refrigerated for 2–3 days.

### Kipper Pâté    Makes 450 g (1 lb)

*335 g (12 oz) kipper, after
    filleting and removing skin
1 small clove garlic*

*45 g (1½ oz) onion, finely
    chopped
90 g (3 oz) butter or margarine
3 teaspoons lemon juice*

If using tinned kipper fillets, add 2 extra teaspoons lemon juice, and 6 teaspoons tomato paste.

Method as in previous recipe.

Suitable for freezing. May be prepared in advance and kept refrigerated for 2–3 days.

## Taramasalata Makes 450 g (1 lb)

*140 g (5 oz) smoked cod's roe*
*3½ tablespoons thin cream*
*5 slices crustless white bread,*
*in milk, squeezed out*
*45 g (1½ oz) onion, finely*
*chopped*

*3 tablespoons olive oil*
*1½ tablespoons lemon juice*
*chopped parsley, or sliced*
*black olives, to garnish*

Soak the smoked cod's roe in milk for 1–2 hours, if very dry. Skin, and blend, preferably in an electric blender, with all other ingredients, till very smooth.

Suitable for freezing. May be prepared in advance and kept refrigerated for 2–3 days.

## Tunafish Pâté Makes 450 g (1 lb)

*370 g (13½ oz) tunafish, with*
*some of its oil*
*20 g (¾ oz) crustless white*
*bread, in water or milk,*
*squeezed out*

*3 tablespoons oil*
*1 teaspoon lemon juice*
*¼ level teaspoon salt*
*black pepper*

Method as in recipe for Smoked Buckling Pâté (page 94).

Suitable for freezing. May be prepared in advance and kept refrigerated for 2–3 days.

## Prawn and Cream Cheese Pâté Makes 450 g (1 lb)

*210 g (7½ oz) shelled prawns*
*or crab*
*210 g (7½ oz) soft cream*
*cheese*

*2 tablespoons liquid, either*
*juice from the tin, or thin*
*cream*
*1 teaspoon tomato paste, to*
*improve the colour (optional)*

Method as in recipe for Smoked Buckling Pâté (page 94).

Not suitable for freezing.

## Horseradish Spread

*20 g (¾ oz) tableready*
*horseradish sauce, mixed*
*with*

*75 g (2½ oz) soft cream cheese*
*2 tablespoons thin cream*

Not suitable for freezing.

### Cream Cheese and Curry Spread

*60 g (2 oz) soft cream cheese,
  mixed with
1 level teaspoon curry powder*

*3 teaspoons chutney
3 tablespoons thin cream*

Not suitable for freezing.

### Cream Cheese and Garlic Spread

*60 g (2 oz) Mayonnaise (page
  69), mixed with*

*60 g (2 oz) soft cream cheese
1 small clove garlic, crushed*

Not suitable for freezing.

### Cream Cheese and Watercress Spread

*60 g (2 oz) soft cream cheese,
  mixed with
2 teaspoons onion, finely
  chopped*

*6 teaspoons watercress, finely
  chopped
3 tablespoons thin cream*

Not suitable for freezing.

### Potted Cheese    Makes 225 g (8 oz)

*110 g (4 oz) cheddar, grated
110 g (4 oz) butter*

*1 tablespoon brandy, medium
  sherry or port
1 teaspoon cumin*

Beat together all ingredients, or mix in an electric blender, till very smooth. Leave for 2 weeks in the refrigerator before using. Spread on savoury biscuits.

### Cheese Spread    Makes 225 g (8 oz)

*60 g (2 oz) cheddar, grated
60 g (2 oz) parmesan, grated
60 g (2 oz) butter*

*2–3 tablespoons cream
pinch cayenne*

Beat together the cheeses and the butter, or mix in an electric blender, till very smooth. Whip the cream, and mix carefully into cheese and butter mixture. Add the cayenne. Pipe on savoury biscuits, or use for filling where a softer consistency is required.

## Herb Cheese    Makes 225 g (8 oz)

*225 g (8 oz) soft cream cheese*
*1 tablespoon fresh lemon*
  *thyme*

*1 tablespoon fresh marjoram,*
*or such herbs as are*
*available, such as chives,*
*borage, parsley, etc., all*
*chopped very finely (dried*
*herbs are not suitable)*

Beat the herbs into the cheese until well blended. Place a fresh bay leaf, if available, or a dried bay leaf, on the base of a dish. Form the cheese into shape like a camembert, and place on the bay leaf. Pour a little olive oil over, and scatter over a few fresh herbs, finely chopped. Leave for 24 hours in a refrigerator before eating.

# 3(d). Hot Canapés and Sandwiches

**EACH RECIPE MAKES 36**

# *Preparation of Bases for Hot Canapés*

### 1. Crouton Bases

There are several methods for preparing croutons (for fillings see pages 102–9):

(a) Cut the bread into pieces of the required size (approximately 3½–4 cm (1½ in) square, or into small rounds or triangles). Place the filling on top and bake on a baking tray in the oven at 200° C (400° F), usually for about 6 minutes. By the time the filling is ready the base will have toasted itself underneath, making a crisp base.

(b) Leave the slices of bread whole, cover with the filling, and bake at 200° C (400° F), usually for about 8–9 minutes. Cut the slice of bread into smaller pieces. The undersides will have toasted themselves, but it is as well to make sure that they are all quite firm, as occasionally the centre of the slice is still a little soft.

(c) Cut the bread into pieces of the required size, and bake at 225° C (435° F) for 3 minutes. They will now be crisp and may be kept in an airtight container for 1–2 days, but no longer.

(d) Toast the slices of bread in the normal way, and cut into smaller pieces. These should be used right away.

(e) Melt a mixture of butter and oil in a frying pan, waiting for the frothing to stop before putting the croutons in the fat. Fry only to a light brown – if too dark they can become very brittle. To make 36 bases use 60 g (2 oz) butter and 2 tablespoons oil. Never fry the slices whole, except in an exceptionally large pan where they can lie flat, as the middle tends to remain soft.

(f) Either cut the slices into smaller pieces, or leave whole, and butter one side. Lay the buttered side down on the baking tray and spread with the filling. The underside will then very lightly fry in the butter while the top is cooking. It makes a very good, firm base, neither as rich as the fried bread, nor as lacking in character as the plain toast.

## 2. Bread Tartlet Shells (for fillings see pages 102–9)

Using a 5 cm (2 in) round cutter, cut out circles from slices of bread. It is more economical to buy an unsliced loaf, and to slice it horizontally, but if in a hurry, it is quicker with a sliced one. Melt 140 g (5 oz) butter in a pan, making sure it stays melted but does not get too hot and start to burn. Using a new 2½ cm (1 in) house painting brush, paint one side of each round of bread with a little butter. In a hurry, melt the butter in a shallow pan and dip each piece of bread directly into the butter. This uses rather more butter. Press each piece of buttered bread firmly into a tartlet baking tin, pressing the middle down very firmly, with the buttered side underneath. Bake at 200° C (400° F) for 8 minutes, or at 250° C (480° F) for 5, or until a light golden brown.

The bread should be cut as thinly as possible. If using a ready-sliced loaf it is as well to roll the bread, after removing the crusts, between damp tea towels before cutting out the rounds. Larger tartlet shells can be made using the 6 cm (2½ in) or 7 cm (2¾ in) cutter.

The shells may be frozen, or prepared a day in advance. To re-heat, spoon in the filling, and re-bake at 200° C (400° F) for about 7 minutes.
Don't fill them more than an hour in advance, or they may go soggy.

## 3. Bread Croustades – Baked (for fillings see pages 110–11)

These are toasted bread cases, about 2 cm (¾ in) deep, cut in squares, rounds or triangles, and hollowed out to hold a filling, rather like a bouchée or vol au vent. The square and triangular shapes are more economical, but the round ones look better. Use a 5 cm (2 in) cutter, and cut out 36 rounds. Take a 4 cm (1½ in) cutter, and laying it centrally over the bread, cut through the bread to about half way down, to cut an inner circle. Lift out this inner circle carefully with the fingers or with the end of a rounded knife blade.

Smaller croustades can be made using a 4 cm (1½ in) cutter, but this is very small. A standard loaf, unsliced, approximately 20 cm (8 in) long should cut into 9 slices at 2 cm (¾ in) after removing the crusts. With careful cutting you should get 4 × 5 cm (2 in) rings from each slice, and easily 4 × 4 cm (1½ in) rings, making 36. Paint the bread with a paint brush dipped in melted butter. 90 g (3 oz) will paint 36 of the 5 cm size. Bake at 225° C (450° F) for 5 minutes.

These may be frozen, or prepared a day in advance and kept in an airtight container. To re-heat, spoon in the filling, and bake at 200° C (400° F), usually for 7 minutes. The filling may be sprinkled with parmesan cheese and a little melted butter before baking. Or it may be re-heated under a moderate grill, unless the filling is very cold, in which case the top may brown before the middle has heated through.

## 4. Bread Croustades – Fried (for fillings see pages 110–11)

Make the croustades as for the baked croustades, but fry in deep fat until a light golden brown. If too dark they will be brittle. Never fry in shallow fat, as the middle doesn't get fried, and stays soggy. Fried croustades stay fresh longer than baked, and can be prepared two or three days in advance and kept in an airtight container.

## 5. Baps (for fillings see pages 102–9)

*225 g (8 oz) plain flour*
*1 teaspoon salt*
*30 g (1 oz) butter or lard*
*7 g (¼ oz) dried yeast (1 level teaspoon)*

*1 level teaspoon sugar*
*1½ dl (¼ pint) milk, warmed to blood temperature*
*½ small egg, mixed with 1 tablespoon milk, for glazing*

Rub the fat into the flour with the fingers, until very fine. Pour the warmed milk into a bowl, mix in the sugar, and sprinkle the dried yeast on top. Stir once and then leave for ten minutes or longer, until it is bubbly and well risen. Make a well in the flour, and pour in the yeast mixture. Mix well, to a soft dough, adding a little extra warm milk or water if necessary. Leave to rise until it has doubled its bulk. This will take at least 2 hours in a warm place. Tip onto a floured board, and knead. Divide the dough into 18 even-sized pieces. Knead each piece into a ball, and flatten slightly. Place on a floured baking tin, and leave to prove for a further 15 minutes, in a warm place, while the oven heats. Brush the tops with the milk and egg mixture and bake for 8–10 minutes, at 170° C (340° F). Cut in half, horizontally, to make 36 halves, to serve as bases. It may be necessary to cut a little off the top of the upper halves, to make them stand steadily.

## 6. Bases using Scone Dough (for fillings see pages 163–5)

See recipe on page 163.

## FILLINGS FOR HOT CANAPÉS

### Mushroom Filling

*30 g (1 oz) onion, finely
chopped or minced
45 g (1½ oz) butter, to fry the
onion
125 g (4½ oz) mushrooms,
finely chopped*

*7 g (¼ oz) plain flour
7 g (¼ oz) butter or margarine,
to make the sauce
4 tablespoons milk
salt and black pepper*

1. Sauté the onion in the butter for 5–10 minutes or till soft. Add the chopped mushrooms and continue for 2–3 minutes more. Make a white sauce (page 68) from the flour, butter or margarine and milk. Mix into the onion and butter mixture, and season.
2. Cover the croutons.
3. Bake at 200° C (400° F) for 6 minutes.

Suitable for freezing or for preparing in advance (see recipe for Chicken Filling, page 103).

### Whole Sautéed Mushrooms

*36 small button mushrooms
(approximately 140 g, 5 oz)
1 tablespoon oil*

*15 g (½ oz) butter
salt and black pepper
1 teaspoon parsley, chopped*

Heat the butter and oil together and sauté the mushrooms, shaking the pan frequently to make sure the mushrooms are covered in the fat, for 3–4 minutes. Season. Lay each mushroom on a crouton, with a cocktail stick to hold it in place. Sprinkle with chopped parsley.

Not suitable for freezing. May be prepared completely in advance, and re-heated at 200° C (400° F) for 5–6 minutes.

### Mushrooms in Garlic Butter

*90 g (3 oz) button mushrooms
30 g (1 oz) butter, or 3
tablespoons olive oil*

*½ clove garlic, crushed
2 teaspoons parsley, chopped
salt and black pepper*

Slice the mushrooms into 4–6 slices each, according to size. Heat the butter or oil with the garlic and sauté the mushrooms for 3–4 minutes. Place 3–4 slices on each crouton and sprinkle with parsley.

Not suitable for freezing. May be prepared completely in advance and re-heated at 200° C (400° F) for 4–5 minutes.

## Chicken Filling

75 g (2½oz) cooked chicken,
  minced
15 g (½oz) plain flour
15 g (½oz) butter or
  margarine

1½ dl (¼ pint) milk
1 small egg yolk
1 tablespoon parmesan
  cheese, grated (optional)
salt and black pepper

1. Make a white sauce with the flour, butter or margarine and milk (page 68). Cool and stir in the egg yolk and add the minced chicken. Season.
2. Spread over the bases, and sprinkle with the parmesan.
3. Bake at 200°C (400°F) for 6–7 minutes.

Suitable for freezing, after completing 1 (see Deep Freezing, page 15). To cook, thaw and continue with 2. Or after 2 (see Deep Freezing, page 15). To cook, thaw on baking trays for 30 minutes and continue with 3. May be prepared in advance to the end of 2 or 3. Continue as above.

## Chicken Liver and Ham Filling

120 g (4¼oz) chicken livers,
  finely chopped
120 g (4¼oz) ham, finely
  chopped or minced
45 g (1½oz) butter

15 g (½oz) plain flour
9 tablespoons stock
½ teaspoon lemon juice
salt and black pepper

1. Heat the butter in the pan and cook the chicken livers very gently for 2–3 minutes only. Add the ham, and then the flour. Stir well. Add the stock and the lemon juice, and stir till a thick sauce is formed. Season.
2. Spread on the bases.
3. Bake at 200°C (400°F) for 6 minutes.

Suitable for freezing or for preparing in advance (see recipe for Chicken Filling above).

## German Beef and Anchovy Filling

This recipe is from Frau Häsi Hugo of Kronberg/Taunus, West Germany.

4 large slices of white or
  brown bread, with crusts on
180 g (6½oz) lean beef,
  minced
6 egg yolks
1 teaspoon dry mustard

large pinch cayenne pepper
2 teaspoons tableready
  horseradish sauce
2 teaspoons brandy (optional)
60 g (2oz) butter or margarine
11–12 anchovy fillets in oil

1. Butter the bread on both sides. Mix all the other ingredients together, except the anchovies, and spread over the bread. Lay the anchovy fillets, cut in thin strips, over the top.
2. Bake at 200°C (400°F) for 10–12 minutes. Cut off the crusts and divide each slice into 9 squares.

Suitable for freezing (see Deep Freezing, page 15). Thaw on baking trays for 20 minutes, and re-heat at 200°C (400°F) for 4–5 minutes. May be prepared in advance to the end of 1. Continue with 2.

## Ham and Pineapple Filling

*75 g (2½ oz) boiled ham, minced or chopped, or in 36 small pieces*

*75 g (2½ oz) pineapple, in 36 small pieces*
*75 g (2½ oz) soft cream cheese*

1. Spread the croutons with the cream cheese, and place a piece of ham, or a little minced ham, over it. Cover with a small piece of pineapple.
2. Bake at 200°C (400°F) for 5–6 minutes. Secure with a cocktail stick to serve.

Not suitable for freezing. May be prepared a few hours in advance to the end of 1. Continue with 2.

## Savoury Choux Pastry Fillings

*3 large tablespoons left-over choux pastry dough*
*1½ tablespoons cream*

*90 g (3 oz) parmesan, grated, or 90 g (3 oz) ham, minced*

1. Soften the left-over dough by placing in a warm bowl, or a bowl over hot water, and beating carefully. Add the cream, and blend together. Add the parmesan or ham. Spread over the croutons (the method using a bread croute buttered on the underside is best).
2. Bake at 225°C (430°F) for 15 minutes.

Suitable for freezing after completing 1. Thaw on baking trays and continue with 2 (see Deep Freezing, page 15). Not suitable for preparing in advance, as the canapés should be cooked and eaten immediately.

## Bacon Fillings

*6 rashers thin bacon (approximately 75 g 2½ oz)*

*various toppings*

1. Cut each rasher into 6, and place one piece on each of the croutons, pressing the bacon well into the bread (the method using plain bread buttered on the underside is best). Lay one of the selected toppings over the bacon.

2. Bake at 200°C (400°F) for 5–7 minutes, according to the ingredients used.

TOPPINGS

A. Scrambled egg – cook the bacon alone on the crouton, add the egg and re-heat 2–3 minutes.

B. Pieces of peach, pineapple or banana – serve with a cocktail stick, to hold in place.

C. Sautéed finely chopped or sliced mushrooms, or sautéed finely chopped red or green peppers.

Not suitable for freezing. May be prepared in advance to the end of 1. Continue with 2.

## Scrambled Egg Fillings

| | |
|---|---|
| *4 large eggs* | *salt and pepper* |
| *40 g (1⅓ oz) butter* | *9–10 anchovy fillets in oil* |

Heat the butter and scramble the eggs until still slightly runny. Place on croutons of fried bread (page 99). Slice the anchovy fillets into thin strips about 3–4 cm (1½ in) long and place over the egg either diagonally, or using two, crossing from the corners. Add a drop of oil from the tin. Re-heat at 200°C (400°F) for 2–3 minutes if the egg was hot, or 4–5 minutes, if re-heating from cold.

VARIATIONS

A. With prawns. To 3 scrambled eggs, add 120 g (4½ oz) finely chopped prawns.

B. With asparagus. To 3 scrambled eggs add 90 g (3 oz) tinned asparagus tips, finely chopped. Sprinkle with parmesan.

C. With red sweet peppers. To 4 scrambled eggs add 90 g (3 oz) finely chopped and fried peppers. Sprinkle with parmesan.

D. With mushroom. To 4 scrambled eggs, chop and sauté 60 g (2 oz) mushrooms and mix with the egg.

E. With ham. To 3 scrambled eggs, add 75 g (2½ oz) minced ham. Garnish with parsley.

F. With tomato and cheese. Skin and de-seed 3 average tomatoes, chop finely and sauté in 15 g (½ oz) butter until all excess juice has boiled away. Add 30 g (1 oz) grated cheddar, 30 g (1 oz) butter and 3 beaten eggs, all together. Stir till setting and season. Add chopped parsley or chopped chives to the mixture, if wished.

G. With crab. Simmer 110 g (4 oz) crab in 45 g (1½ oz) butter. Add ½ teaspoon curry powder, and 3 beaten eggs with 1 tablespoon cream. Scramble all together.

H. With chicken livers. Sauté 110 g (4 oz) finely chopped chicken livers in oil for 2–3 minutes only. In a separate pan, heat 60 g (2 oz) butter and scramble 4 eggs until still slightly runny. Add to the chicken livers, and season. Cover the croutons and re-heat for 2–3 minutes. Sprinkle with chopped parsley.

None of these is suitable for freezing. They may be prepared in advance to the stage of completing the scrambling of the eggs, with additions, but if placed on the croutons too soon they may go soggy. Re-heat by placing on the croutons and baking for 2–3 minutes if the mixture is still warm, and 4–5 minutes if cold.

## Anchovy Filling

*36 croutons measuring 5 cm*        *18 anchovy fillets in oil*
*  by 2½ cm (2 in by 1 in)*         *2 teaspoons parsley, chopped*

1. Cut the anchovies diagonally down their length so that they will fit diagonally across the croutons. Distribute the oil evenly between them.
2. Bake at 200° C (400° F) for 6–7 minutes. Garnish with chopped parsley.

Suitable for freezing after completing 1 (see Deep Freezing, page 15). To re-heat, thaw on baking trays for 20 minutes, and continue with 2. May be prepared in advance to the end of 1. Continue with 2.

## Anchovy and Walnut Filling

*6–7 anchovy fillets in oil,*        *3 teaspoons parsley, chopped*
*  chopped or minced with the*       *½ small clove garlic, crushed*
*  oil*                             *3 tablespoons oil*
*90 g (3 oz) walnuts, finely*        *3 teaspoons lemon juice*
*  chopped*

1. Mix all ingredients together, except the oil and the parsley, and spread on the croutons. Distribute the oil evenly over the canapés.
2. Bake at 200° C (400° F) for 5–6 minutes. Sprinkle with parsley.

Suitable for freezing after completing 1 (see Deep Freezing, page 15). To cook, thaw on baking trays for 30 minutes, and continue with 2. May be prepared in advance to the end of 1. Continue with 2.

## Smoked Salmon or Eel Filling

*90 g (3 oz) smoked eel or
  smoked salmon
3 eggs scrambled with 30 g
  (1 oz) butter (page 111)*

*3 teaspoons chopped dill,
  chives, or parsley (optional)*

1. Cover half the crouton with the scrambled egg, into which you have mixed the chopped herbs if used, dividing the crouton, if square, diagonally from corner to corner. Place a piece of the eel or salmon in the opposite half.
2. Bake at 200° C (400° F) for 4–5 minutes.

Not suitable for freezing. May be prepared an hour or two in advance to the end of 1. Continue with 2.

## Smoked Trout Filling

*170 g (6 oz) smoked trout,
  after skinning and filleting
6 teaspoons cream
6 teaspoons oil*

*1 teaspoon lemon juice
2 teaspoons parsley, chopped
salt and pepper*

1. Mash the trout with the cream and oil. Add the lemon juice, season, and spread on the croutons.
2. Bake at 200° C (400° F) for 5–6 minutes. Garnish with chopped parsley.

Suitable for freezing after completing 1 (see Deep Freezing, page 15). To cook, thaw on baking trays for 30 minutes, and continue with 2. May be prepared in advance to the end of 1. Continue with 2.

## Kipper Filling

*15 g (½ oz) plain flour
15 g (½ oz) butter or
  margarine
1½ dl (¼ pint) milk
60 g (2 oz) kipper, after
  skinning and filleting*

*1 large hard-boiled egg, finely
  chopped
zest of ½ a lemon
3 teaspoons lemon juice
salt and black pepper*

1. Make a white sauce with the flour, butter and milk (page 68). Flake the kipper and add it with the rest of the ingredients to the sauce, mixing well, but taking care not to mash the kipper or egg. Season.
2. Spread on the canapés.
3. Bake at 200° C (400° F) for 6 minutes.

Not suitable for freezing. May be prepared in advance to the end of 1 or 2. Continue as above.

## Sardine Filling

36 croutons 4 cm by 2 cm                    2 tins sardines in oil
  (1½in by ¾in)

1. Split the sardines and carefully remove the backbones, and lay
each half, or piece of suitable size, on the croutons, skin side up.
Distribute the oil from the tin over the canapés.
2. Bake at 200°C (400°F) for 6 minutes.

## Sardine Fingers

36 croutons, 5 cm by 2½cm            60 g (2 oz) cheddar, finely
  (2 in by 1 in)                               grated
90 g (3 oz) sardines                     45 g (1½oz) butter
2 tablespoons fresh white             dash Worcestershire sauce
  breadcrumbs

1. Mash the sardines in their own oil, and spread on the croutons.
Mix the crumbs, grated cheese, Worcestershire sauce and butter
together, and spread over the sardines.
2. Bake at 200°C (400°F) for 6 minutes.

Suitable for freezing after completing 1 (see Deep Freezing, page
15). To cook, thaw on baking trays for 30 minutes and continue with
2. May be prepared in advance to the end of 1. Continue with 2.

## Lobster Filling

30 g (1 oz) butter                        3 teaspoons brandy
90 g (3 oz) lobster                       6 teaspoons cream
60 g (2 oz) mushrooms,               30 g (1 oz) gruyère, grated
  chopped                                     finely
6 teaspoons sherry

1. Simmer the mushrooms in the butter for 2–3 minutes, and add
the lobster. Add the warmed brandy, flame, and simmer for 1–2
minutes more. Add the sherry, turn the heat up and quickly bubble
the liquid for 30 seconds. Add the cream and simmer till thick
enough. Sprinkle with the grated cheese. Spread over the croutons.
2. Bake at 200°C (400°F) for 5–6 minutes.

Not suitable for freezing. May be prepared an hour in advance to the
end of 1. Continue with 2.

## Devilled Crab Filling

75 g (2½ oz) crab
30 g (1 oz) butter
1 tablespoon parmesan
  cheese, grated
1 level teaspoon Dijon
  mustard

6 dashes Worcestershire
  sauce
1 level teaspoon curry powder
salt, black pepper and a pinch
  cayenne pepper

1. Simmer the crab in the butter for 2–3 minutes, and add the other ingredients. Continue to simmer till thick enough.
2. Spread on the croutons. (Garnish, if wished, with a small piece of pineapple or thin slice of banana.) Sprinkle with the parmesan.
3. Bake at 200°C (400°F) for 8–9 minutes.

Suitable for freezing after completing 1 or 2 (see Deep Freezing, page 15). May be prepared in advance to the end of 2. Continue with 3.


## Spanish Prawns with Garlic Filling

120 g (4½ oz) prawns or
  shrimps, after shelling
30 g (1 oz) onion, finely
  chopped

1 small clove garlic, crushed
1 tablespoon oil

1. Simmer the onion in the oil for 5–10 minutes or until soft. Add the prawns or shrimps and the garlic and simmer for 1–2 minutes more. Place on croutons.
2. Bake at 200°C (400°F) for 4 minutes only.


## Prawn Filling

15 g (½ oz) butter
15 g (½ oz) plain flour
1½ dl (¼ pint) milk
1 level teaspoon tomato paste
good pinch paprika

90 g (3 oz) prawns, or other
  shellfish, after shelling,
  chopped
1 egg yolk
2 tablespoons parmesan
  cheese, finely grated

1. Make a white sauce (page 68) with the flour, butter and milk. Add the tomato paste and paprika, then the egg yolk and prawns, mixing well. Spread on the croutons and sprinkle with parmesan.
2. Bake at 200°C (400°F) for 5–6 minutes.

Suitable for freezing and for preparing in advance (see recipe for Chicken Filling, page 103).

# FILLINGS FOR CROUSTADES (for cases see pages 100–101

All these fillings are suitable for freezing, except those containing scrambled or hard-boiled egg. Thaw thoroughly and spoon into the croustades. Sprinkle on the parmesan, if wished, and butter, and bake 7–8 minutes at 200°C (400°F). May be prepared in advance, earlier the same day, and heated for 7–8 minutes at 200°C (400°F).

## Cold      Smoked Haddock Filling

*170 g (6 oz) white fish, or
  smoked haddock, cooked
  and flaked
1½ hard-boiled eggs, finely
  chopped*

*3 rounded dessertspoons
  Mayonnaise (page 69),
  approximately 75 g (2½ oz)
salt and black pepper*

Mix all ingredients together, season, and spoon into the croustades.

## Hot or cold      Crab Filling

*225 g (8 oz) crab
225 g (8 oz) white fish, or use
  all crab
60 g (2 oz) butter
1 tablespoon brandy*

*2 dashes tabasco sauce
3 dl (½ pint) cream
30 g (1 oz) parmesan
45 g (1½ oz) butter
salt and black pepper*

Simmer the crab and fish in the butter, and flame in the brandy. Add the tabasco sauce and cream, and simmer till thick. Season. Spoon into the croustades, sprinkle with the parmesan and melted butter. Bake at 200°C (400°F) for 7–8 minutes.

## Hot or cold      Lobster and Mushroom Filling

*60 g (2 oz) butter, to fry the
  mushrooms and lobster
90 g (3 oz) lobster, crab, or a
  mixture with white fish
120 g (4½ oz) mushrooms,
  sliced very finely
3 tablespoons sherry*

*3 tablespoons thick cream
60 g (2 oz) gruyère, grated
30 g (1 oz) parmesan, grated
45 g (1½ oz) butter, to pour
  over the croustades
salt and black pepper*

Simmer the mushrooms in the butter, add the lobster and white fish, and simmer a further 2–3 minutes. Add the sherry, and boil rapidly for 30 seconds. Add the cream and simmer till thick. Add the gruyère and allow it to melt but not to boil. Season. Spoon into the croustades, sprinkle with the parmesan and butter, and bake at 200°C (400°F) for 7–8 minutes.

Hot or **Scrambled Eggs with Various Additions**
Cold

*6 medium eggs*
*60 g (2 oz) butter*
*salt and black pepper*
*180 g (6¼ oz) minced chicken;*
  *or 90 g (3 oz) shelled prawns*
  *or shrimps, mixed with 90 g*
  *(3 oz) white fish; or 180 g*
  *(6¼ oz) prawns alone; or*
  *140 g (5 oz) bacon, fried*
  *without fat, and crumbled; or*
  *180 g (6¼ oz) finely chopped*
  *and sautéed mushrooms; or*

*110 g (4 oz) tomatoes, skinned*
  *and de-seeded, and*
  *simmered to reduce the*
  *liquid, mixed with 60 g (2 oz)*
  *grated cheese; or 75 g*
  *(2½ oz) chicken livers,*
  *chopped and sautéed, mixed*
  *with 30 g (1 oz) fried and*
  *crumbled bacon; or 120 g*
  *(4 oz) salmon, boiled and*
  *flaked; or 12 finely chopped*
  *anchovy fillets in oil; or*
  *combine two or three of*
  *these ingredients together*

Scramble the eggs and mix in the selected additions. Spoon into the croustades and re-heat for 3–4 minutes at 200° C (400° F).

Hot or **Devilled Crab and Scrambled Egg Filling**
cold

*60 g (2 oz) butter or margarine*
*120 g (4½ oz) crab*
*½ teaspoon curry powder*

*4 large eggs, lightly beaten*
*1 tablespoon cream*
*salt and black pepper*

Melt the butter and sauté the crab 1–2 minutes. Add all other ingredients, stirring all the time, till the eggs scramble, but remain slightly runny. Spoon into the croustades and re-heat at 200° C (400° F) for 7–8 minutes.

Hot or cold **Basic Savoury Sauce**

*60 g (2 oz) butter or margarine*
*30 g (1 oz) plain flour*
*2 dl (⅓ pint) milk*
*just over 1 tablespoon thin*
  *cream*

*salt and black pepper*
*30 g (1 oz) parmesan, grated*
*45 g (1½ oz) butter*

Make a white sauce with the butter, flour and milk (page 68), add the cream and season. Add the selected addition, spoon into the croustades, sprinkle with parmesan and butter and re-heat for 7–8 minutes at 200° C (400° F).

ADDITIONS

225 g (8 oz) mushrooms,
   chopped and sautéed
110 g (4 oz) mushrooms, with
   60 g (2 oz) bacon, fried and
   crumbled
335 g (12 oz) shellfish, or
   mixture of shellfish and
   white fish, or smoked
   haddock

225 g (8 oz) minced ham
450 g (1 lb) minced cooked
   chicken, or turkey
335 g (12 oz) chicken and ham
   mixed
225 g (8 oz) mashed sardines,
   or tunafish
335 g (12 oz) salmon, cooked
   and flaked

# Hot Pinwheels

### Pâté or Sardine Pinwheels

5 slices brown or white bread,
   at least 14 cm (5½ in) in one
   direction

175 g (6½ oz) sardines in oil,
   or strong-flavoured pâté

1. Make the pinwheels as described on page 80, using the sardine or pâté.
2. Bake at 200° C (400° F) for 5 minutes, or toast both sides under a grill.

Suitable for freezing after completing 1 (page 15). Thaw for 30 minutes on baking trays and continue with 2. May be prepared in advance to the end of 1. Continue with 2. Or to the end of 2. Re-heat 2–3 minutes at 200° C (400° F).

### Toasted Cheese Pinwheels

5 slices brown or white bread,
   at least 14 cm (5½ in) in one
   direction

120 g (4½ oz) cheddar, grated
3 level teaspoons prepared
   English mustard
6 tablespoons cream
salt and cayenne pepper

1. Mash together all the ingredients, and spread over the bread. Continue as on page 80.
2. Bake at 200° C (400° F) for 5 minutes, or toast on both sides under a grill.

Suitable for freezing after completing 1 (page 15). Thaw for 30 minutes on baking trays and continue with 2. May be prepared in advance to the end of 1. Continue with 2, but they should not be re-heated once cooked as the cheese will go tough.

## *Hot 'Swiss' Rolls*

### Ham and Asparagus Rolls

bread as in recipe for
  Pinwheels (page 80)
6 slices ham cut very thin
  (approximately 120 g, 4½ oz)

1 teaspoon mustard
asparagus tips

1. Butter the bread generously, lay on the ham, spread with the mustard, lay asparagus tips across from side to side in one line, and roll tightly. Spread a little extra butter on the top. Secure with cocktail sticks.
2. Bake at 200° C (400° F) for 6 minutes, turning the roll over half-way through, as the bottom browns first. Remove the sticks and slice into sections.

Suitable for freezing after completing 1. Thaw on baking trays, and continue with 2. May be prepared in advance to the end of 1. Continue with 2. Or to the end of 2. Re-heat in the rolls for 4–5 minutes, and cut into sections.

### Anchovy or Chicken Liver 'Swiss' Rolls

bread as in the recipe for
  Pinwheels (page 80)
10 anchovy fillets in oil, or
  Chicken Liver Pâté (page 93)

3 teaspoons parmesan
  cheese, grated

1. Butter the bread generously, and lay 2 anchovies across the bottom of each slice of bread. Roll up and secure. Roll in the parmesan. Sprinkle the oil from the tin over the rolls.
2. Lay the rolls join downwards on a baking tray, and bake at 200° C (400° F) for 8 minutes.

Suitable for freezing and for preparing in advance as for the previous recipe.

## *Hot Baby Sandwiches*

### Croque Monsieur

8 large slices white bread,
  with crusts on

4 thin slices ham,
  approximately 85 g (just
  under 3 oz)

4 thin slices gruyère cheese,
approximately 85 g (just
under 3 oz)

½ teaspoon English made
mustard
75 g (2½ oz) butter

Butter the slices of bread and lay the gruyère, spread with the mustard, and the ham, on top. Lay the second slice, butter side down, as for an ordinary sandwich, on top. Press firmly together. Butter the top of the sandwich, and lay it butter side down on a flat frying pan, with no extra fat. Butter the side which is now on top. Heat the pan slowly, and gradually fry the sandwich slowly enough to allow the cheese to melt. Turn over and fry the other side. Cut each sandwich into 9, removing the crusts.

Not suitable for freezing, unless using processed gruyère. May be prepared in advance and re-heated at 200° C (400° F) for 5–6 minutes. It is better to cut into the small sandwiches after reheating.

## Bacon and Mushroom Sandwiches

6 slices white bread, with
crusts on
110 g (4 oz) gruyère, grated; or
any strong flavoured pâté
30 g (1 oz) butter
3 teaspoons oil

20 g (just under 1 oz) bacon,
chopped finely
30 g (1 oz) mushrooms,
chopped finely
1 large egg, mixed with 2
tablespoons milk
4 tablespoons oil for frying

Mash the cheese (or pâté) and butter together and divide between the 6 slices of bread. Fry the chopped bacon in the 3 teaspoons oil, add the mushrooms, and fry gently till cooked. Divide between 3 slices of bread. Cover these with the 3 other slices, and press firmly together. Dip each sandwich quickly, on both sides, in the egg and milk mixture. Fry in the oil slowly, till crisp. Cut off the crusts and cut each into 12 small squares. These are very small, but very rich.

Not suitable for freezing, unless using processed gruyère. May be prepared in advance and re-heated at 200° C (400° F) either as large sandwiches or small for 5–6 minutes.

## Cheese and Mustard Sandwiches

6 slices white bread, with
crusts on
140 g (5 oz) gruyère, grated
1 rounded and 1 level
tablespoon Mayonnaise
(page 69), 90 g (3 oz)

1 tablespoon English made
mustard
1 large egg, mixed with 2
tablespoons milk

As for the previous recipe, mixing the cheese with the mayonnaise and mustard, and dipping in the egg and milk mixture.

Not suitable for freezing, but may be prepared in advance and re-heated, as for previous recipe.

# 4

# PASTRIES

## 4(a). Shortcrust Pastries

**EACH RECIPE IS FOR 36 PASTRIES UNLESS OTHERWISE STATED**

Hot or cold          **Sausage Rolls**

*shortcrust pastry dough (page 175) using 90 g (3 oz) plain flour (i.e. one-third quantities given)*

*225 g (8 oz) sausagemeat
1 small egg mixed with 1 teaspoon water*

1.  Roll the dough till it measures 38 cm by 33 cm (15 in by 13 in) with the pastry lying with the longer length across the board. Divide the meat into 4. Roll each piece into a long sausage, the same length as the pastry, and spread evenly along the top edge of the dough, leaving 2½ cm (1 in) free at the top. Leave another 2½ cm (1 in) free in front of the meat, and then, with a pastry brush wet the next 2½ cm (1 in) with water. Roll the top of the pastry over the sausagemeat, and roll both over until they overlap the wet area. This should have used up a quarter of the pastry. Cut the pastry all the way along just in front of the roll. Roll it backwards and forwards a few times, to help to seal the join, then turn it on its back, and press the join again with a fork or flat blade of a knife. Turn it on its front, and with a very sharp knife make small diagonal slashes across the top of the roll. Cut away any untidy ends, and cut the roll into 9 pieces. Repeat, to make 3 more rolls. You should now have 36 very small sausage rolls. Paint with a little egg and water mixture, to brown the top.
2.  Place in the oven at 250° C (480° F) for 7–8 minutes.

Suitable for freezing (a) after completing 1. To cook thaw on a baking tray for 30 minutes, and continue with 2. Or (b) after completing 2. Re-heat for 5–6 minutes at 200° C (400° F). May also be prepared in advance, as above. They will keep in the refrigerator or in an airtight tin for several days.

Hot or cold      **Apple and Sausage Rolls**

*125 g (4½ oz) sausagemeat*
*110 g (4 oz) very thick apple*
*  sauce*

*shortcrust pastry dough (page*
*  175) using 90 g (3 oz) plain*
*  flour (i.e. one-third quantities*
*  given)*
*1 small egg mixed with 1*
*  teaspoon water*

1. and 2. As for Sausage Rolls (see previous recipe) spreading the
apple sauce on the pastry under the sausagemeat.

Suitable for freezing and for preparing in advance, as for Sausage
Rolls.

Hot or cold      **Chicken and Ham Rolls**

*shortcrust pastry dough (page*
*  175) using 90 g (3 oz) plain*
*  flour (i.e. one-third quantities*
*  given)*
*110 g (4 oz) soft cream cheese*

*110 g (4 oz) minced chicken*
*110 g (4 oz) minced ham*
*60 g (2 oz) chopped tinned*
*  pineapple*
*1 small egg mixed with 1*
*  teaspoon water*

1. As for Sausage Rolls (page 118), substituting the cheese, chick-
en, ham and pineapple for the sausagemeat.
2. Bake at 225°C (450°F) for 18 minutes.

Suitable for freezing and for preparing in advance, as for Sausage
Rolls.

Hot or cold      **Sausage and Salami Rolls**

*shortcrust pastry dough (page*
*  175) using 90 g (3 oz) plain*
*  flour (i.e. one-third quantities*
*  given)*
*110 g (4 oz) sausagemeat*
*60 g (2 oz) salami, chopped*
*  very finely*

*110 g (4 oz) stuffed olives,*
*  chopped finely*
*60 g (2 oz) red sweet pepper,*
*  chopped finely*
*1 small egg mixed with 1*
*  teaspoon water*

1. As for Sausage Rolls (page 118), substituting the mixture of
sausagemeat, salami, stuffed olives and peppers, for the
sausagemeat alone. Roll as for sausage rolls, but do not cut into
sections. Paint with the egg and water mixture.
2. Bake in the long rolls, at 225°C (450°F) for 14–15 minutes. Cut
each roll into 9 sections, tidying away any untidy ends.

Suitable for freezing or preparing in advance, as for Sausage Rolls.

Hot                    **Bacon and Chicken Liver Pasties**

*shortcrust pastry dough (page      12 rashers very thin bacon*
*175) using 90 g (3 oz) plain          (approximately 170 g, 6 oz)*
*flour (i.e. one-third quantities    1 small egg mixed with 1*
*given)                                 teaspoon water*
*140 g (5 oz) chicken livers*

1. Cut the rashers each into 3 and stretch slightly, lengthwise.
Divide the livers into 36 pieces (this is much easier if the livers have
been frozen, and are just beginning to thaw), and wrap a piece of
bacon round each. Continue as for Sausage Rolls (page 118), placing 9 bacon and chicken liver rolls in place of each long roll of
sausagemeat. Do not cut into sections. Paint with the egg and water
mixture.
2. Bake the long rolls at 200°C (400°F) for 20 minutes, but if after
10–12 minutes the pastry is browning too quickly, reduce the heat,
as the chicken livers must have the full 20 minutes. Cut between the
rolls, cutting away any untidy ends.

Suitable for freezing, as for Sausage Rolls, unless the chicken livers
were previously frozen, in which case they should be cooked before
being re-frozen. May also be prepared in advance.

# *Tartlets*

## **Method and Deep Freezing**

*215 g (7½ oz) plain flour          2 egg yolks*
*125 g (4½ oz) butter or            2 pinches salt*
*margarine                          1 or more tablespoons water*
*60 g (2 oz) cheese, very finely*
*grated*

This is a rich pastry and gives extra flavour to the tartlets. It is
particularly useful for using when baking tartlets with the filling
inside, as opposed to baking 'blind'. But the recipe for shortcrust
pastry (page 175) is also suitable, and can be used instead, if
preferred.

Sieve the flour and salt into a large bowl, and mix in the butter or
margarine, cut in very small pieces, using thumbs and fingertips;
mix in the finely grated cheese. Add the egg yolks and 1 tablespoon
water, and mix with a knife. Add a little more water if necessary, until
it all amalgamates and forms a ball. Turn out onto a floured board
and knead gently till smooth. Rest for at least 30 minutes in a cool
place before using.

Divide the dough into 2, and roll each piece to 38 cm by 19 cm (15 in by 7½ in) for easier handling. Cut a total of 36 circles with a 6 cm (2½ in) cutter. Place in special baking trays for round-bottomed tartlets, fill, and bake for the time specified in each recipe. There are several other shapes of baking tin available which can be used, with fillings, instead of the plain round, or the baby quiche shape. Quantities of both pastry and filling may have to be slightly adapted. The shell-shaped tins are particularly appropriate for shell-fish fillings.

The pastry is suitable for freezing, or for preparing in advance, and storing in a polythene bag, or in foil, in the refrigerator for 4–5 days. The cooked tartlets are also suitable for freezing, or for preparing in advance and storing in an airtight container for 2–3 days. But they are very much better if they can be served at once, or re-heated later on the day on which they were cooked. It is sometimes necessary to replace the cooked tartlets in the baking tins for re-heating. Bake for 6–7 minutes at 200°C (400°F), after thawing for 1 hour.


## FILLINGS FOR TARTLETS


Hot or cold　　**Mushroom or Prawn Filling**

*125 g (4½ oz) chopped mushrooms, or 170 g (6 oz) prawns, sautéed in a little oil and butter*
*30 g (1 oz) butter or margarine*
*30 g (1 oz) flour*
*just over 3 dl (½ pint) milk*

*1 medium egg, lightly beaten*
*salt and black pepper*
*30 g (1 oz) parmesan cheese, grated*
*30 g (1 oz) butter, melted, to pour over the tartlet filling*

Make a white sauce with the butter or margarine, flour, milk and seasonings (page 68). Add the beaten egg, and mix well. Sauté the mushrooms or prawns in the oil and butter. Add to the sauce mixture. Spoon the mixture into the uncooked tartlet shells, sprinkle over the parmesan and pour a few drops of butter into each. Bake at 200°C (400°F) for 18–20 minutes.


Hot　　　　**Pissaladière Filling**

An adaptation from an old Provençale recipe.

*360 g (13 oz) onion, finely chopped*
*6 tablespoons olive oil*

*125 g (4½ oz) soft cream cheese*
*8 anchovy fillets*
*24 black olives*

Sauté the onions in the olive oil. Stir in the cream cheese until well mixed. Spoon into the uncooked tartlet shells. Slice the anchovy fillets very thinly into 36 pieces, and lay across the top of each tartlet. Stone and slice the black olives into 4–5 slices each, and distribute them over the tartlets. Bake at 200°C (400°F) for 17–18 minutes.

Hot                              **Anchovy Filling**

Another adaptation from a Provençale recipe.

*450 g (1 lb) tomatoes*           *black pepper*
*6 tablespoons olive oil*         *8 anchovy fillets*
*1 clove garlic, crushed*         *125 g (4½ oz) soft cream*
*pinch fresh basil if possible,*    *cheese*
  *or dried*

Skin the tomatoes in boiling water, and de-seed them. Sauté them in the oil, until most of the water has evaporated, and they are simmering in the oil. Add the garlic, basil and pepper. Spoon the mixture into uncooked tartlet shells. Slice the cream cheese thinly and lay on top of the tomato. Slice the anchovy fillets very thinly into 36 pieces and lay across the top of each tartlet. Bake at 200°C (400°F) for 17–18 minutes.

Hot                        **Cheese and Salami Filling**

*3 eggs, lightly beaten*          *170 g (6 oz) salami, cut in very*
*170 g (6 oz) cheddar or*           *small cubes*
  *gruyère cheese, finely grated*

Mix all ingredients together and spoon into uncooked tartlet shells. Bake at 200°C (400°F) for 14–15 minutes.

Hot                           **Rich Gruyère Filling**

*25 g (¾ oz) butter or*           *3 eggs, well beaten*
  *margarine*                     *140 g (5 oz) gruyère, finely*
*25 g (¾ oz) plain flour*           *grated*
*3 dl (½ pint) milk*              *salt and black pepper*
*2 tablespoons cream*             *pinch cayenne pepper*

Make a thick white sauce using the butter or margarine, flour and milk (page 68). Add the cream and mix well. Add the eggs and mix well. Stir in the gruyère and seasonings. Spoon into the tartlet shells. Bake at 200°C (400°F) for 19–20 minutes.

Hot or cold       **Bacon and Egg Filling**

*30 g (1 oz) bacon (or chicken),*
  *finely chopped*
*30 g (1 oz) onion, finely*
  *chopped*
*110 g (4 oz) mushroom,*
  *chopped*

*30 g (1 oz) butter or margarine*
*1½ tablespoons parsley,*
  *chopped*
*1½ eggs, lightly beaten*
*5 tablespoons cream*
*salt and black pepper*

Cook the bacon or chicken, onion and mushrooms in the butter and add the parsley. Mix the egg with the cream, salt and pepper, add the mushroom mixture, and spoon into uncooked tartlet shells. Bake at 200° C (400° F) for 10 minutes.

# *Baby Quiches*

## Method and Deep Freezing

*Shortcrust pastry dough (page*
  *175) using 255 g (9 oz) plain*
  *flour*

These are baked in straight-sided baking tins, with a 5 cm (2 in) base. You can use an 8 cm (3¼ in) cutter or a 7 cm (2¾ in) cutter. The first gives a slightly deeper quiche, and all quantities are given for that size. If you prefer a shallower quiche use the 7 cm (2¾ in) cutter, and use three-quarters of the quantity of filling given.

Divide the dough into 2 pieces, for easier handling. Roll each piece to approximately 50 cm by 25 cm (20 in by 10 in) of very thin pastry. (This gives a very high proportion of filling to pastry. If you prefer the pastry to be thicker, or find it difficult to manage as thin as this, increase the quantity of pastry by using 335 g (12 oz) plain flour, 225 g (8 oz) very cold margarine, 2½–3 tablespoons very cold water and ¾ teaspoon salt.) Using an 8 cm (3¼ in) cutter, cut 18 circles from each piece of pastry. Lift each one and carefully press into the baking tins. The sides will fall into folds, which won't show in the cooked quiche. If you wish you can cut round the top of each quiche with a very sharp knife to even the edge, but this isn't really necessary. Fill with the selected filling and bake at 200° C (400° F) for 26–28 minutes.

All these baby quiches are suitable for freezing. They should be thawed for 45 minutes, and re-heated at 200° C (400° F) for 7–8 minutes. They may also be prepared in advance, and stored in an airtight container for 2–3 days. But they are better eaten on the day they were cooked, and re-heated if necessary.

## FILLINGS FOR BABY QUICHES

Hot or cold          **Baby Mushroom Quiches**

*100 g (3½ oz) onion, chopped*
*45 g (1½ oz) butter or*
  *margarine*
*365 g (13 oz) mushrooms*
*2 medium eggs and 1 yolk,*
  *lightly beaten*

*3 dl (½ pint) less 2*
  *tablespoons cream*
*30 g (1 oz) gruyère cheese,*
  *grated*
*30 g (1 oz) butter*
*salt and black pepper*

Simmer the onions in the butter or margarine for 5–10 minutes or till soft, add the mushrooms and continue till cooked. Season. Spoon into the shells. Mix the cream with the beaten eggs, and divide between the shells. Sprinkle the grated cheese over the egg mixture, and place a small piece of butter on each shell. Bake at 200°C (400°F) for 26–28 minutes.

Hot or cold          **Baby Quiches Lorraine**
                 (Cream and Bacon Quiche)

*110 g (4 oz) thin bacon*
*2 medium eggs and 1 yolk*
*3 dl (½ pint) less 2*
  *tablespoons cream*

*30 g (1 oz) gruyère cheese,*
  *grated (optional)*
*30 g (1 oz) butter*
*salt and black pepper*

Cut the bacon into small pieces and distribute between the shells. Mix the cream with the beaten eggs, salt and pepper, and pour into the shells. Sprinkle the grated cheese over the egg mixture, and place a small piece of butter on each shell. Bake at 200°C (400°F) for 26–28 minutes.

Hot or cold          **Baby Quiches a la Niçoise**
                     (Tomato Quiche)

*30 g (1 oz) onions, finely*
  *chopped*
*500 g (18 oz) tomatoes,*
  *skinned and de-seeded*
*1 small clove garlic*
*½ teaspoon dried oregano,*
  *basil or thyme*
*salt and black pepper*

*1 medium egg and 2 yolks,*
  *beaten together*
*8 anchovy fillets*
*3 tablespoons olive oil*
*30 g (1 oz) gruyère cheese,*
  *grated*
*1 tablespoon olive oil to pour*
  *over the quiches*

Simmer the onions, tomatoes, garlic and herbs in the 2 tablespoons olive oil, until most of the water has evaporated and the mixture is thick. Season. Cool. Stir in the egg and yolks. Spoon the mixture into the shells. Cut the anchovy fillets into small pieces and spread over the tomato mixture. Sprinkle a little cheese into each quiche and pour over a few drops olive oil. Bake at 200° C (400° F) for 26–28 minutes.

### Hot or cold  **Baby Spinach and Ham Quiches**

*45 g (1½ oz) onion, finely chopped*
*1¼ tablespoons oil*
*90 g (3 oz) frozen, chopped spinach, after removing all water*
*90 g (3 oz) ham, finely chopped*

*salt and black pepper*
*2 medium eggs and 1 yolk, beaten together*
*3 dl (½ pint) cream less 2 tablespoons*
*30 g (1 oz) gruyère cheese, grated*
*30 g (1 oz) butter*

Simmer the onion in the oil for 5–10 minutes or until soft. Stir in the spinach, ham, beaten eggs and cream. Season. Spoon the mixture into the shells. Sprinkle a little cheese into each quiche and then a small piece of butter. Bake at 200° C (400° F) for 26–28 minutes.

### Hot or cold  **Baby Leek Quiches**

*400 g (14 oz) leeks*
*3 dl (½ pint) salted water*
*salt and black pepper*
*45 g (1½ oz) butter*
*2 medium eggs and 1 yolk*

*3 dl (½ pint) less 2 tablespoons cream*
*30 g (1 oz) gruyère cheese, grated*
*30 g (1 oz) butter*

Chop the leeks finely across the stems, and soak in clean water to remove any grit. Simmer in the salted water till tender. Drain off the water, add the butter, and braise gently till they have formed a thick sauce. Add the eggs and cream, and season. Spoon into the uncooked shells. Sprinkle a little gruyère into each quiche, and then a small piece of butter. Bake at 200° C (400° F) for 26–28 minutes.

### Hot or cold  **Baby Asparagus Quiches**

*225 g (8 oz) tinned asparagus tips*

All other ingredients as for Baby Leek Quiches (previous recipe), omitting the salted water, unless using fresh asparagus, and continue in the same way.

## Baby Tuna and Anchovy Quiches

Hot or cold

285 g (10 oz) tunafish
3 dl (½ pint) less 2
  tablespoons cream

two medium eggs and 1 yolk,
  beaten together
1 small tin anchovy fillets in
  oil

Flake the tunafish finely, and mix with the cream and eggs. Spoon into the shells. Cut the anchovy fillets into thin strips, and criss-cross over the shells. Pour over the oil. Bake at 200°C (400°F) for 26–28 minutes.

Hot or
cold

## Baby Onion Quiches with Black Olives

400 g (14 oz) onions, chopped
  finely
45 g (1½ oz) butter
1 tablespoon olive oil
20 g (¾ oz) plain flour
2 small eggs, beaten together
7 tablespoons cream

salt and black pepper
45 g (1½ oz) gruyère cheese,
  grated
1 tablespoon oil, to pour over
  the shells
20 black olives

Simmer the onions in a mixture of butter and oil. Stir in the flour and cream mixed together, and bring carefully back to the boil until the flour has just thickened. Cool. Stir in the eggs, and season. Spoon into the shells, sprinkle a little gruyère cheese into each shell, and a few drops olive oil. Stone the black olives, slice each into 4 or 5 slices, and distribute over the shells. Bake at 200°C (400°F) for 26–28 minutes.

Hot

## Baby Gruyère Quiches

2 medium eggs and 1 yolk,
  beaten together
3 dl (½ pint) less 2
  tablespoons cream

¼ teaspoon salt and pinch
  black pepper
110 g (4 oz) gruyère cheese,
  grated
30 g (1 oz) butter

Mix together the eggs, cream and seasoning. Divide the gruyère between the shells, and pour over the egg and cream mixture. Put a small piece of butter in each shell. Bake at 200°C (400°F) for 26–28 minutes.

Hot or cold    **Baby Prawn Quiches**
(or Fruits de Mer)

*45 g (1½ oz) onions, finely*
  *chopped*
*45 g (1½ oz) butter*
*110 g (4 oz) prawns, or crab,*
  *or lobster, etc., or a mixture*
  *of shellfish and white fish*
*2 tablespoons white wine*
  *(optional)*

*2 medium eggs*
*7 tablespoons cream*
*1 teaspoon tomato paste*
*pinch paprika*
*salt and black pepper*
*30 g (1 oz) gruyère cheese,*
  *grated*
*30 g (1 oz) butter*

Simmer the onions for 5–10 minutes in the butter, or until soft. Add the shellfish, and simmer for a further 2–3 minutes. Add the wine, if using it, raise the heat and bubble it hard, till almost evaporated. Cool. Add the tomato paste and paprika, and the eggs mixed with the cream. Spoon into the shells, sprinkle with a little gruyère, and put a small piece of butter in each shell. Bake at 200° C (400° F) for 26–28 minutes.

Hot or    **Baby Salami and Cream Cheese Quiches**
cold

*30 g (1 oz) onion, chopped*
  *finely*
*30 g (1 oz) butter*
*1 large egg, lightly beaten*
*3 dl (½ pint) less 2*
  *tablespoons cream or milk*
*75 g (2½ oz) soft cream cheese*
*2 teaspoons parsley, chopped*

*½ teaspoon dried oregano*
*salt and black pepper*
*60 g (2 oz) salami, in small*
  *cubes*
*⅓ green sweet pepper, finely*
  *chopped (optional)*
*30 g (1 oz) butter*

Simmer the onion in the butter for 5–10 minutes, or until soft. Mash the cream cheese, gradually add the cream or milk and the egg, and add to the onion. Season. Distribute the salami in the shells, and pour the onion mixture over. Sprinkle with the parsley and oregano and add the green pepper if using it. Place a small piece of butter in each shell. Bake at 200° C (400° F) for 26-28 minutes.

# Pre-cooked Tartlet Shells

## Method and Deep Freezing

Shortcrust pastry dough (page 175) using three-quarters of the quantity given, that is, using 190 g (6¾ oz) flour. Or make the full quantity and use the remainder to make Shortcrust Biscuits (page 145).

Divide the dough in half for easier handling. Roll each half to approximately 38 cm by 19 cm (15 in by 7½ in). This makes a very thin pastry. If you prefer a thicker shell, use the full quantity of dough, that is, 255 g (9 oz). Cut 18 circles from each with a 6 cm (2¼ in) cutter. Bake 'blind', that is, without filling, by placing in round-bottomed baking tins, pricking them all over very gently with a fork, placing small pieces of foil of about the same size over the pastry, and placing a few dried beans on top to hold the foil in place and prevent the pastry rising. Bake for 9 minutes at 200° C (400° F). They tend to shrink a little.

Suitable for freezing. They may also be prepared in advance and stored in an airtight container for a few days.

## HOT FILLINGS

All the following fillings may be prepared in advance and used to fill pre-cooked tartlet shells. After filling, pour a few drops of butter over, and sprinkle with a little parmesan cheese, if wished. Bake at 200° C (400° F) for 6–7 minutes, to re-heat. Except for those containing egg, the hot fillings can be deep frozen and used to fill pre-cooked shells before being re-heated as above.

## Chicken and Mushroom Filling

*30 g (1 oz) onion, chopped
  finely
30 g (1 oz) butter, to sauté the
  onion
150 g (5 oz) cooked chicken,
  chopped or minced
150 g (5 oz) mushrooms, or
  sweet red peppers, or water
  chestnuts, chopped and
  sautéed in 45 g (1½ oz) butter*

*4 tablespoons white wine
30 g (1 oz) plain flour
30 g (1 oz) butter, to make the
  sauce
3 dl (½ pint) milk or stock
1 egg yolk
4 tablespoons cream
salt and black pepper*

Sauté the onions in the butter for 5–10 minutes or until soft. Add the chicken and mushrooms (or peppers or chestnuts), and continue for another 4–5 minutes. Add the wine, raise the heat, and bubble the wine until it has almost all evaporated. Add the second quantity of butter, and when it is hot, sprinkle over the flour carefully so as to prevent lumps forming. When it is well mixed in add the milk all at once, and stir until a thick sauce has formed. Continue to simmer for a further 2–3 minutes. (If you prefer, make the white sauce (page 68) separately, and add to the chicken and vegetable mixture.) Cool a little, add the egg yolk, mix in, and add the cream. Season.

### Rich Shellfish Filling

*170 g (6 oz) prawns, chopped*
*170 g (6 oz) whitefish, cooked*
*and flaked*
*90 g (3 oz) butter*

*1 tablespoon brandy*
*2 tablespoons dry sherry*
*12 tablespoons cream*
*salt and black pepper*

Simmer the fish in the butter. Add the brandy, warmed, and set fire to it. Simmer for a further 1–2 minutes. Add the sherry, raise the heat to make it bubble, and continue until most of the liquid has evaporated. Stir in the cream. Season. Continue to simmer till thick enough to spoon into the shells.

### 'Hot' Chicken Filling

*335 g (12 oz) chicken,*
*chopped, or a mixture of*
*chicken and ham, etc.*
*90 g (3 oz) butter*

*6 dashes tabasco*
*12 tablespoons cream*
*salt*

As for previous recipe, using the tabasco in place of the brandy and sherry.

### Chicken and Mushroom in Ginger

*170 g (6 oz) chicken breast,*
*uncooked*
*4 rounded teaspoons*
*cornflour*
*45 g (1½ oz) crystallized*
*ginger, cut very finely*
*45 g (1½ oz) onion, chopped*

*2 tablespoons oil*
*1 tablespoon marsala or sweet*
*sherry*
*3 tablespoons stock*
*2 tablespoons cream*
*salt and black pepper*

Cut the chicken in thin strips across the grain, and then into little pieces, and toss in the cornflour. Fry the onion gently in the oil for 5–10 minutes or till soft, and add the chicken and ginger. Cook the chicken till it turns white. Add the marsala or sherry, raise the heat and bubble till almost evaporated. Add the stock, and when thick, add the cream and continue to simmer till thick enough.

### Spanish Prawns in Garlic

*170 g (6 oz) prawns, finely*
*   chopped*
*45 g (1½ oz) onion, finely*
*   chopped*

*1 clove garlic, crushed*
*2 tablespoons oil or olive oil*
*salt and black pepper*

Sauté the onions in the oil for 5–10 minutes or till soft, adding the garlic towards the end. Add the prawns and continue for 1 minute more. Season.

### Prawns in Tomato Sauce

*170 g (6 oz) prawns, chopped*
*90 g (3 oz) cucumber, peeled*
*   and finely chopped*
*30 g (1 oz) onion, finely*
*   chopped*
*30 g (1 oz) red sweet pepper,*
*   finely chopped*

*2 tablespoons oil*
*3 teaspoons tomato ketchup*
*3 teaspoons cornflour*
*10 tablespoons milk*
*1 small egg yolk*
*salt and black pepper*

Simmer the onion, cucumber and peppers for 5–10 minutes in the oil, or till soft. Add the prawns, and continue for 1 minute more. Sprinkle on the cornflour carefully, and add the ketchup and milk, and stir continually until it thickens. Simmer for 2–3 minutes. Cool. Add the egg yolk, mix well, and heat until it thickens, but do not re-boil. Season.

### Scrambled Egg Fillings

As for filling Croustades (page 111). Reheat for only 3–4 minutes.

Not suitable for freezing.

## Chicken Livers Filling

45 g (1½ oz) onion, chopped
1 tablespoon oil
110 g (4 oz) chicken livers,
  chopped
90 g (3 oz) mushrooms,
  chopped
280 g (10 oz) tomatoes,
  skinned and de-seeded

2 teaspoons parsley, chopped
3 tablespoons white wine or
  good stock
1 level teaspoon cornflour,
  mixed in 1 tablespoon stock
salt and black pepper

Sauté the onion for 5–10 minutes or till soft. Add the chicken livers, and simmer 3–4 minutes. Add the mushrooms, and continue to simmer 1 minute more. Add the tomatoes, parsley, white wine or stock, and simmer till reduced to a thin sauce. Add the cornflour in the extra stock, and stir till thickened. Season.

## Devilled Roes and Mushroom Filling

45 g (1½ oz) onions
170 g (6 oz) soft roes, chopped
170 g (6 oz) mushrooms,
  chopped
60 g (2 oz) butter
3 tablespoons oil
¼ level teaspoon paprika

1 teaspoon curry powder
6 tablespoons thin cream or
  milk
pinch cayenne
salt and black pepper

Sauté the onions in the oil for 5–10 minutes or till soft. Add the butter, and when hot add the mushrooms, paprika and curry powder. Simmer for 2–3 minutes. Add the roes, simmer for a further 2–3 minutes. Add the cream, stirring, and simmer till thick enough. Season with the salt, black pepper and cayenne.

## Asparagus in Hollandaise Sauce Filling

200 g (7 oz) asparagus tips
335 g (12 oz) Hollandaise
  Sauce (page 68),
  approximately 6 tablespoons

2 teaspoons parsley, chopped

Drain and dry the asparagus tips. Lay them carefully in the shells, and spoon the sauce over. They should be served immediately, sprinkled with chopped parsley. Alternatively, they can be mixed into the sauce before spooning into the shells.

Not suitable for freezing.

## Kipper and Egg Filling

20 g (¾ oz) plain flour
20 g (¾ oz) butter or
  margarine
2 dl (⅓ pint) milk
120 g (4¼ oz) kipper, after
  skinning and boning

3 hard-boiled eggs, finely
  chopped
zest of 1 lemon
3 teaspoons lemon juice
salt and black pepper

Make a white sauce from the flour, butter or margarine and milk (page 68). Flake the kipper, and add to the sauce, with the lemon zest and juice and the chopped hard-boiled eggs.

Not suitable for freezing.

## Tuna and Anchovy Filling

150 g (5½ oz) tunafish, plus a
  little of its oil
35 g (1¼ oz) plain flour
35 g (1¼ oz) butter or
  margarine
3 dl (½ pint) milk

4 teaspoons parsley and
  chives together, chopped
2 teaspoons lemon juice
2½ tablespoons thin cream or
  milk
12 fillets anchovies in oil
salt and pepper

Flake the tuna finely, but don't mash. Make a white sauce with the flour, butter or margarine and milk (page 68). Add the cream to the sauce. Add the tunafish, parsley and lemon juice, mix carefully, and spoon into the shells. Cut the anchovies very thinly and lay criss-cross over the top of the filling.

## COLD FILLINGS

None of the following fillings is suitable for freezing. They may be prepared in advance and used to fill pre-cooked tartlet shells, served cold. In recipes using soft cream cheese the amount of liquid needed to soften the cheese varies slightly according to the different cheeses, and also with the temperature. If the mixture is prepared in a warm kitchen, and then refrigerated overnight, it will become much thicker. It may, therefore, be necessary to add a little extra milk or cream just before filling the shells and serving.

## Salmon and Cucumber Filling

*170 g (6 oz) soft cream cheese*
*4 tablespoons thin cream or*
  *milk*
*240 g (8½ oz) salmon, after*
  *removing skin and bones (or*
  *use tunafish in place of the*
  *salmon), flaked*

*60 g (2 oz) cucumber, peeled*
  *and chopped finely*
*salt and black pepper*

Blend the cheese and cream together and add the salmon and cucumber

## Avocado and Tunafish Filling

*170 g (6 oz) soft cream cheese*
*6 tablespoons milk*
*170 g (6 oz) Avocado and*
  *Tunafish Dip (page 71)*

*salt and black pepper*
*chopped parsley, or*
  *hard-boiled egg, to garnish*

Blend the cheese and milk together and spoon into the shells. Pour 1 large teaspoon dip into each shell. Garnish with chopped parsley or hard-boiled egg.

## Kipper and Tomato Filling

*125 g (4½ oz) soft cream*
  *cheese*
*3 tablespoons milk or cream*
*3 small kippers, approximately*
  *200 g (7 oz) after removing*
  *skin and bones*

*170 g (6 oz) tomatoes, after*
  *skinning and de-seeding*
*salt and black pepper*

Blend the cheese and milk or cream together, and add the kipper, flaked, and chopped tomatoes; or place all ingredients in an electric blender, and make a thick purée. Spoon into the shells.

## Sardine and Olive Filling

*75 g (2½ oz) soft cream cheese*
*2½ tablespoons milk or cream*
*200 g (7 oz) sardines*
*7 teaspoons lemon juice*
*4 teaspoons parsley, chopped*

*14 stuffed olives, chopped, or*
*2 tablespoons celery, finely*
  *chopped*
*salt and black pepper*

Blend the cheese and milk or cream together, mash the sardines with the lemon juice, and blend with the cheese mixture. Add the rest of the ingredients.

## Cream Cheese and Bacon Filling

240 g (8½ oz) soft cream
  cheese
6 tablespoons thin cream or
  milk

170 g (6 oz) bacon, fried and
  crumbled
salt and black pepper

Blend the cheese and cream together and mix in the bacon. Season.

## Celery, Apple and Nut Filling

300 g (11 oz) soft cream
  cheese
10 tablespoons thin cream or
  milk
60 g (2 oz) celery, finely
  chopped

60 g (2 oz) apple, finely
  chopped
60 g (2 oz) walnuts, finely
  chopped
salt and black pepper

Blend the cheese and cream together, and add the celery and apple
and seasoning. Spoon into the shells. Sprinkle the chopped walnuts
over.

## Ham and Celery Filling

170 g (6 oz) soft cream cheese
3 tablespoons milk
30 g (1 oz) onions, finely
  chopped

60 g (2 oz) celery, finely
  chopped
90 g (3 oz) ham, minced or
  finely chopped
salt and black pepper

Blend the cheese and milk together and add all the other ingredients.

## Turkey and Pimento Filling

140 g (5 oz) soft cream cheese
5 tablespoons thin cream or
  milk
140 g (5 oz) turkey, or chicken,
  minced

110 g (4 oz) red or green sweet
  pepper, blanched if fresh,
  and finely chopped
1½ tablespoons Chilli Sauce
  (page 67)
salt and black pepper

Blend the cheese and cream together, and add all the other ingredients.

## Blue Cheese and Walnuts

*140 g (5 oz) soft cream cheese*
*12 tablespoons thin cream or*
  *milk*

*140 g (5 oz) blue cheese*
*36 half-walnuts, or 90 g (3 oz)*
  *chopped*
*salt and black pepper*

Blend together the cream and the cheeses. Season. Spoon into the shells. Garnish with either one half-walnut, or with chopped walnuts.

## Mayonnaise Filling

Mayonnaise (page 69)
A. *to 5 tablespoons add 225 g (8 oz) chopped prawns. Garnish with paprika.*
B. *to 3½ tablespoons add 110 g (4 oz) chopped prawns and 140 g (5 oz) asparagus tips, drained, and dried and chopped. Garnish with chopped parsley.*
C. *to 4 tablespoons add 140 g (5 oz) chopped prawns (or prawns and white fish mixed), 75 g (2½ oz) chopped apple, 60 g (2 oz) chopped celery, and garnish with paprika.*
D. *to 4 tablespoons add 170 g (6 oz) prawns, 7 chopped gherkins and 2 teaspoons capers. Garnish with paprika.*

## Paprika Mayonnaise Fillings

Paprika Mayonnaise (page 70)
A. *to 4 tablespoons add 3 hard-boiled eggs, chopped. Garnish with chopped parsley or chives.*
B. *to 5 tablespoons add 200 g (7 oz) prawns. Garnish with sliced stuffed olives.*
C. *as in C in the Mayonnaise section.*
D. *to 4 tablespoons add 75 g (2½ oz) prawns and 75 g (2½ oz) raw mushrooms, sliced. Garnish with chopped walnuts.*

## Curry Mayonnaise Fillings

Curry Mayonnaise (page 70)
A. *to 5 tablespoons add 200 g (7 oz) chopped prawns. Garnish with chopped pineapple.*
B. *to 4 tablespoons add 3 hard-boiled eggs, chopped. Garnish with finely chopped onion or chives.*
C. *to 5 tablespoons add 170 g (6 oz) minced chicken or turkey, 60 g (2 oz) finely sliced raw mushrooms and 60 g (2 oz) finely chopped celery. Garnish with small pieces of tinned peach.*

### Aioli fillings

Aioli (page 71)
*to 5 tablespoons add 200 g (7 oz) assorted vegetables (chopped
cucumber, celery, gherkins, peas, radishes, sliced raw mushrooms,
etc.); or fruits (apple, pineapple, etc.); with prawns, chicken, ham,
mussels, hard-boiled egg, etc., all in small pieces.*

## Egg Mayonnaise Fillings

8 tablespoons Mayonnaise (page 69), mixed with 5 finely chopped
hard-boiled eggs.
Garnish with:
A. *black or red lumpfish caviare.*
B. *sliced black or stuffed olives.*
C. *chopped chives.*

Or mix 3 medium eggs with:
A. *140 g (5 oz) smoked white fish, garnished with parsley.*
B. *140 g (5 oz) filleted and boned kipper, garnished with parsley, and
a squeeze of lemon juice.*

## Scrambled Eggs

To 6 eggs scrambled in 60 g (2 oz) butter (page 111) add:
A. *110 g (4 oz) prawns.*
B. *150 g (5 oz) drained and dried asparagus tips.*
C. *180 g (6 oz) fried and crumbled bacon.*
D. *125 g (4½ oz) grated cheddar, 4 teaspoons tomato ketchup, and
garnish with chopped parsley.*
E. *60 g (2 oz) grated cheddar, 4 teaspoons tomato ketchup and 90 g
(3 oz) crab.*

## Crab or Tunafish Mousse

| | |
|---|---|
| *125 g (5 oz) crab meat or* | *2 teaspoons gelatine* |
| *tunafish* | *4 tablespoons water* |
| *90 g (3 oz) soft cream cheese* | *2 egg whites* |
| *2 egg yolks* | *salt and black pepper* |
| *2 teaspoons lemon juice* | |

Place the crab meat or tunafish, cream cheese, egg yolks and lemon
juice in an electric blender and mix till smooth. Dissolve the gelatine
in the hot water. Cool slightly, and add to the blender. Season and
mix again. Turn into a bowl and leave to cool. When on the point of
setting whisk the egg whites and add to the mixture. Either spoon
the mixture at once into the shells, in which case the mixture will set

flat, or wait a little longer till almost set, and pipe into the shells in whirls. If flat, garnish with a little mayonnaise, sprinkled with parsley, or if in whirls, with parsley alone.

## Savoury Mousse

*1½ dl (¼ pint) tinned double consommé*
*½ clove garlic*

*½ level teaspoon curry powder (or up to 1 teaspoon for stronger flavour)*
*250 g (9 oz) soft cream cheese*

Place all ingredients in an electric blender and mix till smooth. Fill pastry shells as in the previous recipe. Garnish with chopped parsley or chives.

## Salmon or Ham Mousse

*170 g (6 oz) fresh boiled, or tinned salmon, after removing all skin and bones; or ham*
*30 g (1 oz) butter or margarine*
*30 g (1 oz) plain flour*

*3 dl (½ pint) good salmon or fish stock; or ham stock if using ham*
*1 level teaspoon tomato purée*
*2 small eggs or 1 large*
*¾ dl (⅛ pint) cream*
*1 level tablespoon gelatine*
*salt and black pepper*

Make a sauce using the butter, flour and stock, as for white sauce (page 68), reserving 2–3 tablespoons stock for the gelatine. Add the flaked salmon (or finely chopped ham), egg yolks, tomato purée and gelatine dissolved in the stock, and mix together, or place all ingredients into an electric blender if a very smooth mousse is required. Whip the cream, and add to the mixture, and season. Whip the egg whites and add to the mixture. Either fill tartlets at once, or leave till almost set (see Crab Mousse page 136). If filling at once, garnish with mayonnaise, and finely chopped cucumber or parsley, or if in whirls, with parsley.

Hot or cold   ## *Little Shortcrust Pies*

### Method and Deep Freezing

*Shortcrust pastry dough (page 175) using 335 g (12 oz) plain*

*flour (i.e. one-third more than quantities given)*

Divide the dough into 4 for easier handling. Roll each piece to approximately 38 cm by 19 cm (15 in by 7½ in). This makes very thin pastry. Cut 18 circles from each, with a 6 cm (2¼ in) cutter. Lay half the circles in round-bottomed baking tins, put in the filling, dampen the edges with water, and lay the other half on top. Press round the edges with the prongs of a fork or the blade of a small knife to ensure they are sealed. Paint the tops with milk or a mixture of 1 egg and 1 teaspoon water, to help to brown them. Bake for approximately 17 minutes at 200° C (400° F).

It is possible to make very tiny pies, using the quantity of short-crust dough on page 175, rolling the dough into 4 pieces, each approximately 30 cm by 15 cm (12 in by 6 in), and cutting the circles with a 5 cm (2 in) cutter; they are more difficult to make, and hold only half the amount of fillings as the 6 cm pies, so that the pastry proportion tends to be rather high. But they look very good indeed, and if you want to try them, use the same fillings, always using half the quantity. They should be baked 12–13 minutes at 200° C (400° F).

All little shortcrust pies are suitable for freezing and for preparing in advance. Re-heat at 200° C (400° F) for 8–9 minutes.

Hot or cold    **Sausage Meat Pies**

Shortcrust pastry dough, as for Little Shortcrust Pies (page 137). Method, see above, to make 36 bases with a 6 cm (2¼ in) cutter.

For the filling:

| | |
|---|---|
| 170 g (6 oz) sausagemeat | 6 teaspoons parsley, chopped |
| 1 tablespoon oil | salt and black pepper |
| 90 g (3 oz) mushrooms | 1 small egg mixed with 1 |
| ¼ teaspoon lemon juice | teaspoon water |

This is allowing for good quality sausagemeat. If rather flavourless, add 6 teaspoons Chilli Sauce (page 67).

1. Fry the meat gently in the oil for 5 minutes, add the mushrooms, and fry till cooked. Add the lemon juice, chopped parsley and season.
2. Continue as for Little Shortcrust Pies (see above).

Hot or cold **Curry Pies**

Shortcrust pastry dough, as for Little Shortcrust Pies (page 137).

For the filling:
*30 g (1 oz) onion, finely chopped*
*2 tablespoons oil*
*1 small apple, grated*
*60 g (2 oz) sultanas*
*1 level tablespoon curry powder*
*15 g (½ oz) plain flour*

*2 level tablespoons tomato ketchup, or red currant jelly, or sieved apricot jam*
*285 g (10 oz) cooked chicken, minced*
*just over 3 dl (½ pint) stock*
*1 small egg mixed with 1 teaspoon water*

1. Simmer the onion in the oil, add the curry powder and the flour, and stir well. Add the stock and the ketchup, and make into a thick sauce. Add the grated apple and the sultanas, simmer for a further 1–2 minutes.
2. Continue as for Little Shortcrust Pies (page 137).

Hot or cold **Little Provençal Pies**

Shortcrust pastry dough, as for Little Shortcrust Pies (page 137).

For the filling:
*45 g (1½ oz) bacon, in thin rashers*
*60 g (2 oz) onion, finely chopped*
*170 g (6 oz) mushrooms, finely chopped*
*1 tablespoon oil or olive oil*

*6 teaspoons parsley, chopped*
*3 egg yolks, beaten together*
*8 tablespoons thin cream (1½ dl, ¼ pint)*
*1 small egg mixed with 1 teaspoon water*

1. Fry the bacon, cut into small pieces, add the oil and the onions, sauté till soft, add the mushrooms and continue to sauté till cooked. Add the parsley, and the cream. Stir in the egg yolks over a low heat, so that they thicken but do not boil.
2. Continue as for Little Shortcrust Pies (page 137).

Hot or cold **Little Shellfish Pies**

Shortcrust pastry dough, as for Little Shortcrust Pies (page 137).

For the filling:
*255 g (9 oz) shellfish, or a mixture of shellfish and whitefish, cooked and flaked*
*45 g (1½ oz) butter*
*45 g (1½ oz) plain flour*

*3 dl (½ pint) milk*
*yolk of 1 egg*
*1 level teaspoon tomato paste*
*pinch paprika*
*salt and black pepper*

1. Make a white sauce with the butter, flour and milk (page 68). Stir in the egg yolk, shellfish, paprika and tomato paste.
2. Continue as for Little Shortcrust Pies (page 137).


Hot or cold                    **Pirogs**
                    (Three- or Four-sided pies)

Shortcrust pastry dough (page 175) using:
*170 g (6 oz) plain flour*          *1½ tablespoons very cold water*
*90 g (3 oz) very cold margarine*   *¼ teaspoon salt*

1. Cut the dough into two, and roll each piece to approximately 45 cm by 23 cm (17½ in by 9 in) making very thin pastry. Cut 18 squares from each (6 × 3) at 7 cm (2¾ in) square. These form four-sided pirogs.
  Or; cut the dough into 2, and roll each piece to approximately 38 cm by 19 cm (15 in by 7½ in) and cut 18 squares from each (6 × 3) at 6 cm (2¼ in) square. These look very attractive, but are difficult for a beginner to handle. These form very small four-sided pirogs.
  Or; cut the dough into 2, and roll each piece to approximately 45 cm by 23 cm (17½ in by 9 in) and cut 18 circles from each, using a 7 cm (2¾ in) cutter. These circles hold the same amount of filling as the 6 cm squares, but are three sided, like a pyramid.
2. Fill the pirogs with one of the following fillings, placing a tea-spoonful in the centre of the larger, and a very small teaspoonful in the centre of the smaller. All quantities are for the smaller four-sided pirog or the three-sided pirog. To fill the larger, allow half as much filling again as in the recipes.
(a) Four-sided pirogs. Bring the four corners up to meet in the middle, in a point, and press firmly together. Then press firmly together the sides which have as a result become adjacent. A more reliable join is made if the pastry is made slightly damp first, but don't overdo this.
(b) Three-sided pirogs. Place two fingers and a thumb at three equidistant places round the circle, and bring the pastry up to meet in the centre. Press the centre joins firmly together, and then press together the sides which have now become adjacent. As with the four-sided pirogs, slightly damp pastry makes a more reliable join.
  In both cases, paint with milk, or an egg and water mixture, to help the pastry to brown.
  Bake at 200°C (400°F) for 12–13 minutes for the small pirogs, and 16 minutes for the larger.

All pirogs are suitable for freezing and for preparing in advance. Re-heat at 200°C (400°F) for 8–9 minutes. The larger ones may require a little longer.

## FILLINGS FOR PIROGS

### Salmon and Tunafish Filling

*20 g (¾ oz) butter*
*20 g (¾ oz) plain flour*
*10 tablespoons milk*
*45 g (1½ oz) gruyère cheese*

*½ egg yolk*
*90 g (3 oz) tunafish, mashed*
*  into its oil; or salmon*
*salt and black pepper*

1. Make a white sauce with the butter, flour and milk (page 68). Cool and add the egg yolk, the grated cheese and the fish. Mix well, and season.
2. Continue as for recipe for Pirogs (page 140).

### Greek Chicken Filling

*225 g (8 oz) minced cooked*
*  chicken*
*15 g (½ oz) plain flour*
*15 g (½ oz) butter or*
*  margarine*
*6 tablespoons strong chicken*
*  stock*

*1 tablespoon cream*
*½ large or 1 small egg yolk*
*generous pinch Greek rigani,*
*  or Italian oregano, or thyme*
*salt and black pepper*

1. Make a white sauce with the butter or margarine, flour and stock and cream (page 68). Add the chicken, and the egg yolk. Cook gently till the yolk thickens, but don't allow to boil. Add the herbs and seasoning.
2. Continue as for recipe for Pirogs (page 140).

Hot or cold  ## *Shortcrust Pinwheels*

*Shortcrust pastry dough (page*
*  175) using 90 g (3 oz) plain*
*  flour (i.e. one-third quantities*
*  given)*

1. Divide the dough into 2 pieces. Roll each piece out to just over 20 cm (8 in) square. Spread each piece with one of the following fillings. Roll over the near end, and roll tightly to the far end. Damp the last 2 cms and press firmly to seal.
2. Tidy away any untidy edges, and cut each roll into 18 slices, making 36.
3. Bake at 200° C (400° F) for 7–8 minutes.

# FILLINGS FOR SHORTCRUST PINWHEELS

A. *45 g (1½ oz) anchovy paste, sprinkled over with 2 teaspoons chopped parsley.*

B. *45 g (1½ oz) finely minced uncooked bacon, mixed with 30 g (1 oz) sautéed chopped mushrooms, and 1 tablespoon chopped parsley. The bacon cooks as the pinwheel bakes.*

C. *75 g (2½ oz) soft cream cheese mashed with 30 g (1 oz) anchovy paste.*

D. *110 g (4 oz) bel paese cheese, with a pinch cayenne.*

E. *110 g (4 oz) grated cheddar, mashed with ½ a beaten egg, and a pinch cayenne.*

F. *125 g (4½ oz) sardines mashed with 1 teaspoon lemon juice and a little of the oil.*

Suitable for freezing, (a) after completing 1. Thaw for 1 hour, and continue with 2 and 3. Or (b) after completing 3. Thaw for 15 minutes and re-heat at 200° C (400° F) for 3–4 minutes. May be prepared in advance to the end of 3 and stored in an airtight container for several days. Re-heat at 200° C (400° F) for 3–4 minutes, or serve cold.

Hot or cold  ## Shortcrust Turnovers

### Method and Deep Freezing

Shortcrust pastry dough (page 175) using three-quarters of the quantity given, that is, using 190 g (6¾ oz) flour. Or make the full quantity and use the remainder to make Shortcrust Biscuits, page 145.

METHOD 1

Divide the dough in 2, and roll each piece to approximately 36 cm by 18 cm (14 in by 7 in). Using a 6 cm (2¼ in) fluted cutter, cut 18 circles from each (6 × 3). Damp one half of the diameter, place the filling to one side of the centre, bring the other side over to meet, and press down firmly all the way round to seal. Paint the tops with an egg and water mixture. Bake at 225° C (430° F) for about 8 minutes.

METHOD 2

Use the full amount of pastry, divide into 2, and roll each piece to approximately 45 cm by 22 cm (17½ in by 8½ in) and cut 18 circles at 7 cm (2¾ in). These are rather large. Continue as for Method 1.

METHOD 3

Use the full amount of pastry, and divide it into 4 pieces. Roll each piece to just over 30 cm by 15 cm (12 in by 6 in), and cut 72 circles with a 5 cm (2 in) cutter. Place the filling in the centre of half the circles, damp the edges all the way round, and place the other half of the circles on top to make little flat pies. Press well to seal. Paint the tops with an egg and water mixture, and bake at 225° C (430° F) for 8 minutes.

All turnovers are suitable for freezing before cooking (see Deep Freezing, page 15). Thaw for 45 minutes on baking trays, and bake for 7–8 minutes at 200° C (400° F). They may also be prepared completely in advance, and stored in the refrigerator. Re-heat for 7–8 minutes at 200° C (400° F).

## SHORTCRUST TURNOVER FILLINGS

Quantities given are for the 6 cm (2¼ in) Turnover (Method 1). Allow half as much again for Method 2 or 3.

Hot or cold       **Pâté and Mushroom Filling**

*140 g (5 oz) pâté, e.g. Chicken*          *30 g (1 oz) butter*
  *Liver (page 93)*                        *salt and black pepper*
*140 g (5 oz) mushrooms, finely*
  *chopped*

1. Sauté the mushrooms in the butter. Season. When cool mix with the pâté.
2. Continue as in the recipe for Shortcrust Turnovers, page 142.

Hot or cold       **Cheese and Bacon Filling**

*90 g (3 oz) bacon, chopped*               *2 dashes tabasco, or a good*
  *and fried*                                *pinch cayenne pepper*
*3 tablespoons cream*                      *1 level teaspoon curry powder*
*120 g (4 oz) emmenthal or*                *1 large egg, lightly beaten*
  *gruyère cheese, grated*                 *salt and black pepper*
*¼ level teaspoon dry mustard,*
  *mixed with a little of the*
  *cream*

1. Mix all ingredients till well blended. Season.
2. Continue as in the recipe for Shortcrust Turnovers, page 142.

Hot or cold                **Curry Filling**

*90 g (3 oz) cooked, minced*        *1 level tablespoon curry*
  *chicken, or chopped prawns*        *powder*
*1 tablespoon chutney*             *½ teaspoon lemon juice*
*just over 1 tablespoon plain*      *60 g (2 oz) sultanas, chopped*
  *flour*                          *7 tablespoons stock*
*30 g (1 oz) butter or margarine*   *salt and black pepper*

1. Make a white sauce from the butter or margarine, the flour and
the stock (page 68), using stock instead of milk. Add the rest of the
ingredients and mix well.
2. Continue as in the recipe for Shortcrust Turnovers, page 142.

Hot or cold        **Spanish Prawn Filling**

*190 g (7 oz) shelled prawns or*    *1 clove garlic, crushed*
  *shrimps*                         *2 tablespoons oil or olive oil*
*60 g (2 oz) onion, finely*         *good pinch paprika*
  *chopped*                        *salt and black pepper*
*2 large teaspoons tomato*
  *purée*

1. Fry the onion gently in the oil with the garlic for 5–10 minutes or
till soft. Add the prawns and simmer for 1 minute more. Add the rest
of the ingredients. Season.
2. Continue as in the recipe for Shortcrust Turnovers, page 142.

Hot or cold   **Bacon and Chicken Liver Filling**

*60 g (2 oz) butter or margarine*   *60 g (2 oz) bacon, in thin*
*60 g (2 oz) plain flour*             *rashers, chopped*
*4½ dl (¾ pint) milk*              *90 g (3 oz) chicken livers,*
*1 large egg yolk or 2 small*        *chopped, or 110 g (4 oz)*
*90 g (3 oz) gruyère cheese*         *minced cooked chicken*
                                  *salt and black pepper*

1. Make a white sauce with the butter or margarine, flour and milk
(page 68). Add the egg yolk, and heat very gently until it thickens, but
do not allow it to boil. Stir in the cheese off the heat, and do not
re-cook. Sauté the bacon in its own fat, and add the chicken or
chicken livers. Fry for 3–4 minutes. Add to the sauce mixture.
Season.
2. Continue as in the recipe for Shortcrust Turnovers, page 142.

# *Shortcrust Biscuits*

*Left-over shortcrust dough*

Cut the biscuits from pieces of left-over dough, using a very small cutter. Prick them with the prongs of a fork, and bake at 200°C (400° F) for 5–6 minutes. Spread with a savoury butter, and garnish, or use as the base for any of the cold canapé recipes.

Suitable for freezing. May be prepared in advance and stored in an airtight container for several days. After spreading with a filling it will become soft after more than a few hours.

# 4(b). Cheese Pastries

**EACH RECIPE IS FOR 36 PASTRIES UNLESS
OTHERWISE STATED**

Cold            **Cheese Straws and Biscuits**
          Makes approximately 40 straws or 60 biscuits

*Cheese shortcrust pastry
  dough (page 175) using half
  the quantities given. Use
  more margarine if a richer
  pastry is required.*

Roll the pastry to approximately 38 cm by 19 cm (15 in by 7½ in). Cut thin strips, to make straws, about 7½ cm by less than 1 cm (3 in by ⅓ in).

To make the biscuits, in various shapes:
1. Use a 2½ cm (1 in) cutter, and cut rounds. Prick over before baking.
2. Use a 4 cm (1½ in) cutter. Cut circles, and place on one side. Then lay the cutter over approximately half of one of the circles, and cut through it. This divides the original circle into two, making a crescent shape and an oval shape. By varying the position of the cutter different sizes can be made. Prick over before baking.
3. Bake at 200°C (400°F) for 10–12 minutes. Make sure that they don't brown too much, as over-cooked cheddar takes on a bitter taste.

VARIATIONS

A. Paint the straws, before cutting, and the biscuits, with an egg and water mixture, and sprinkle with parmesan cheese.

B. After baking, the 2½ cm (1 in) biscuits can be placed on top of each other, with a cream cheese or other filling in between.

C. After baking, the 4 cm (1½ in) biscuits can be spread with a savoury butter, and garnished, or used as a base for a cold canapé (see Section 3a).

Cold          **Cheese Butterflies**

*36 cheese biscuits at 4 cm*      *36 biscuits at 2½ cm (1 in)*
*  (1½ in)*                   *cheese filling for Stuffed*
                             *Sausages (page 29)*

Pipe some of the cheese filling onto the centres of the larger biscuits. Cut the smaller biscuits in half, and place, with cut edge down, into the filling, at 45 degrees from the base, like a pair of butterfly's wings. Pipe extra filling between the wings, and garnish with a little paprika.

Hot or         **Cheese Sausage Rolls**
cold

Use the recipe for Sausage Rolls (page 118), substituting cheese pastry for shortcrust pastry.

Hot or      **Cheese Apple and Sausage Rolls**
cold

Use the recipe for Apple and Sausage Rolls (page 119), substituting cheese pastry for shortcrust pastry.

Hot or      **Cheese Sausage and Salami Rolls**
cold

Use the recipe for Sausage and Salami Rolls (page 119), substituting cheese pastry for shortcrust pastry.

Warm or cold         **Cheese Sablés**

*60 g (2 oz) flour*                *¼ level teaspoon salt*
*60 g (2 oz) butter*              *pinch cayenne pepper*
*60 g (2 oz) cheddar, grated*

Rub the butter into the flour and add the cheese, salt and cayenne, but as this quickly becomes very sticky, due to the high proportion of butter to flour, use a knife as far as possible. Then tip the mixture onto a well-floured board, and knead with well-floured hands. Leave in the refrigerator to harden for an hour at least. Line baking dishes with foil, as the butter is liable to burn. Roll the dough to just over 30 cm by 15 cm (12 in by 6 in) and cut into 18 squares of about 5 cm (2 in). Cut these squares across to make 36 triangles. Bake for 8 minutes at 180° C (350° F). Sprinkle with a little parmesan or paprika immediately on removing from the oven. Leave to cool a little, as they are very brittle.

May be prepared in advance, and stored in an airtight tin, and re-heated, but they are very much nicer eaten straight away.


Warm or cold          **Walnut Sablés**

Ingredients as for Sablés in the previous recipe, plus:

*1 small egg mixed with 2*          *30 g (1 oz) parmesan, grated*
  *teaspoons water*                 *salt*
*45 g (1½ oz) walnuts, crushed*
  *(or salted peanuts)*

Mix the ingredients, and roll out the pastry as in the previous recipe. Paint over the pastry with the egg and water mix, using a 2½ cm (1 in) house-painting brush, and sprinkle with the walnuts or peanuts and parmesan. If using walnuts, sprinkle also a little salt. Continue as in previous recipe. Any left-over pastry may be re-rolled and cut and baked, rolling in any nuts, and painting again with the egg and water mixture, and sprinkling on any surplus parmesan.

May be prepared in advance, as for Sablés.


Hot or cold    **Cheese and Anchovy Fingers**

*Cheese shortcrust pastry*          *60 g (2 oz) (2 tins) anchovy*
  *(page 175), using half the*       *fillets in oil*
  *quantities given*

Roll the dough to approximately 30 cm by 23 cm (12 in by 9 in). Cut into 4 strips, 23 cm by 7½ cm (9 in by 3 in). Then lay strips of anchovies across the narrow width, at 2½ cm (1 in) intervals, allowing 9 to a piece of pastry. Paint over the pastry and anchovies with the egg and water mixture, and cut between the anchovies. Bake at 200° C (400° F) for 5–6 minutes.

May be prepared in advance and stored in an airtight container for a day or two. Re-heat at 200° C (400° F) for 3–4 minutes, or serve cold.

Hot or cold     **Sardine Turnovers**

*Cheese shortcrust pastry*     *5–6 sardines*
*dough (page 175), using*
*one-third of the quantities*
*given*

1. Use the method described for Cheese Shortcrust Pastry (page 175), using the above quantities. Divide the dough in half, and roll each half, to approximately 38 cm by 19 cm (15 in by 7½ in) and cut 18 circles from each with a 6 cm (2¼ in) cutter. Mash the sardines in their own oil, and place a small amount to one side of the centre of each round. Damp the edge half-way round, and bring one side over to meet the other, forming a letter D. Press edges firmly together, decorating with fork prongs, or a knife blade if wished.
2. Bake at 225°C (435°F) for 6 minutes.

Suitable for freezing after completing 1, and may be packed directly into containers if well dusted with flour to prevent sticking. Thaw on a baking tray for 30 minutes, paint with egg and water mixture, if wished, and continue with 2. May be completely prepared a day or two in advance, and re-heated at 200°C (400°F) for 3–4 minutes.


Warm or cold     **Cheese Wafers**

*60 g (2 oz) plain flour*     *salt and pinch cayenne*
*225 g (8 oz) gruyère,*     *pepper*
*emmenthal or other hard*     *1 small egg mixed with 1*
*cheese, finely grated*     *teaspoon water*
*225 g (8 oz) butter*     *35 g (1¼ oz) hard cheese,*
    *finely grated, to sprinkle over*

1. Mix the flour, grated cheese and butter together. Take a teaspoonful in well-floured hands, and roll into a little ball, flatten it till it is 1 cm (⅓ in) thick.
2. Paint with the egg and water mixture. Repeat with the rest of the mixture. Sprinkle with the finely grated cheese, and bake at 170°C (340°F) for 3–4 minutes only. These are very delicate, lacy wafers.

Suitable for freezing after completing 1, and may be packed at once into containers if well covered in flour. Thaw for 20 minutes on a baking tray and continue with 2. May be prepared completely in advance and stored for a few days in an airtight container. Re-heat at 200°C (400°F) for 2–3 minutes if they have gone soft.

Hot or cold        **Cheese Pastry Tartlets**

*Cheese shortcrust pastry          full quantity and use the*
  *dough (page 175), using 190 g  remaining dough to make*
  *(6¾ oz) flour, or make the      Cheese Biscuits (page 146).*

Method and Fillings as for Shortcrust Tartlet Shells (page 128).


Cold        **Cream Cheese and Fruit Filling**

*180 g (6¼ oz) soft cream          6 tablespoons milk*
  *cheese                          various garnishes*

Mash the cream cheese and gradually blend in the milk. Spoon into
the cold shells. Garnish with black or green grapes, de-seeded and
quartered, arranged in a star shape, or pieces of pineapple, peach or
tinned pear. Or use less cream cheese and milk and mix the fruit into
the filling.

Not suitable for freezing. The filling may be prepared in advance, but
the shell should only be filled an hour or two in advance.

# 4(c). Puff Pastries

## (All served hot)

**EACH RECIPE IS FOR 36 PASTRIES**

---

All the recipes are for home-made puff pastry. Very good ready-made pastry is easily available and can be used instead. When the recipe suggests making home-made pastry with 450 g (1 lb) flour, you should use ready-made pastry weighing 900 g (2 lb). In other words, double the weight of the flour.

## Bouchées

*Puff pastry dough (page 176)*
 *using the full quantity*

1.  Divide the dough in half. Roll the first half to just over 25 cm (10 in) square. Cut out 36 circles (6 × 6) with a 4 cm (1½ in) cutter, fluted or plain. Lay these on a wet baking tray, and damp the edges. Cut 36 similar circles from the other piece of dough. With a 2½ cm (1 in) cutter, cut out the centres. Lay the circles on top of the bases, pressing gently to seal them together. Lay the centres on wet baking

trays also. (These will form the lids. You may prefer to have the bouchées open, in which case there is no need to bake the lids.)
2. Brush the surfaces with a mixture of egg and water. Bake at 230°C (450°F) for approximately 14 minutes. Just before they are ready remove them from the oven and with a sharp, pointed knife blade cut round the inside of the well, and pull out with a finger a little of the centre. Return the bouchées to the oven and bake for a further 2–3 minutes, to dry out the base.

Suitable for freezing (a) after completing 1 (see Deep Freezing, page 15). Thaw on baking trays for 30 minutes and continue with 2. Or (b) after completing 2. Thaw for 20 minutes, and re-heat at 200°C (400°F) for 4–5 minutes. May be completely prepared in advance and stored for a few days in an airtight container. Re-bake for 3–4 minutes at 200°C (400°F) if they have gone soft.

## FILLINGS FOR BOUCHÉES

Fill the bouchée cases, replace lid if wished, and re-heat 7–8 minutes at 200°C (400°F). Or fill the bouchée cases, sprinkle with 30 g (1 oz) parmesan cheese and 30 g (1 oz) melted butter, and do not replace the lid. Re-heat for 7–8 minutes at 200°C (400°F).

### Basic Simple Recipe for Fillings

*30 g (1 oz) butter*           *1 tablespoon cream*
*30 g (1 oz) plain flour*      *salt and black pepper*
*7 tablespoons milk*

Make a white sauce from the butter, flour and milk (page 68). Add the cream and seasoning. Add whatever additions you want:

A. *110 g (4 oz) mushrooms, finely chopped and sautéed*
B. *110 g (4 oz) prawns, shelled and chopped*
C. *110 g (4 oz) sweetbreads, cooked and chopped*
D. *125 g (4½ oz) chicken or turkey, cooked and minced*
E. *90 g (3 oz) boiled ham, minced*
F. *90 g (3 oz) sardine, mashed*
G. *125 g (4½ oz) salmon, cooked, or tunafish, both flaked*

Suitable for freezing or preparing a day in advance and refrigerating.

## Basic Rich Recipe for Fillings

*1½ teaspoons onion, chopped finely*
*15 g (½ oz) butter for the onions*
*1½ tablespoons dry white wine*
*1½ teaspoons parsley or fresh herbs, finely chopped (optional)*

*15 g (½ oz) butter for the sauce*
*15 g (½ oz) plain flour*
*7 tablespoons milk*
*7 tablespoons thin cream*
*½ small egg yolk*
*salt and black pepper*

See previous recipe for suggested additions.

Fry the onions gently in the butter for 5–10 minutes or until soft. Add the wine, raise the heat and bubble the wine for 30 seconds. Add the herbs, if using them. Add the rest of the butter, and carefully sprinkle in the flour. Stir well till smooth. Add the milk and stir till it thickens into a very thick sauce. Add the egg yolk mixed into the cream, and stir carefully allowing the yolk to thicken, but the sauce should not boil again. Add any of the additions from the previous recipe. Season.

Suitable for freezing or preparing a day in advance and refrigerating.

## Scrambled Egg Fillings

As for Croustades (page 111), using the same quantities.

## Prawns and Hollandaise Sauce Filling

As for Asparagus in Hollandaise Sauce Filling (page 131), substituting prawns for asparagus.

## Cheese Filling

As for Savoury Éclairs (page 158).

## Puff Pastry Sausage Rolls

Puff Pastry dough (page 176) using:
*90 g (3 oz) plain flour*
*good pinch salt*
*90 g (3 oz) very cold margarine*

*few drops lemon juice*
*3 tablespoons very cold water*

Method as for Shortcrust Sausage Rolls (page 118).
Suitable for freezing and for preparing in advance as for Shortcrust Sausage Rolls.

## Puff Pastry Apple and Sausage Rolls

Puff pastry dough (page 176), using the same quantities as previous recipe.

Method and freezing as for Shortcrust Apple and Sausage Rolls (page 119).

## Puff Pastry Sausage and Salami Rolls

Puff pastry dough (page 176), the same quantities as the last two recipes.

Method and freezing as for Shortcrust Sausage and Salami Rolls (page 119).

## Puff Pastry Little Pies

Puff pastry dough (page 176) using:
*250 g (9 oz) plain flour*          *1½ dl (¼ pint) very cold water*
*½ level teaspoon salt*            *1 teaspoon lemon juice*
*250 g (9 oz) very cold margarine*

Divide the dough into 4 pieces. Roll each piece to just over 30 cm by 15 cm (12 in by 6 in). Cut 18 circles from each (6 × 3) using a 5 cm (2 in) cutter. Continue as in the recipe for Shortcrust Pies (page 137). All fillings for Shortcrust Pies are suitable for Puff Pastry Pies. As these are smaller, use only half the quantities given. Bake for 8–9 minutes at 225° C (435° F).

All puff pastry pies are suitable for freezing and for preparing in advance. Re-heat at 200° C (400° F) for 8–9 minutes.

## Puff Pastry Turnovers

Puff pastry dough (page 176) using:
*90 g (3 oz) plain flour*          *few drops lemon juice*
*good pinch salt*                  *3 tablespoons very cold water*
*90 g (3 oz) very cold margarine*

Divide the dough in 2 and roll each piece to just over 36 cm by 18 cm (14 in by 7 in). Using a 6 cm (2¼ in) cutter, cut 18 circles, (6 × 3) from each. Continue as for Method 1, Shortcrust Turnovers (page 142). Puff Pastry Turnovers may be painted with an egg and water mixture and baked at 225° C (435° F) for 8–9 minutes. They may also be deep-fried at 200° C (400° F) until golden brown. Drain on absorbent paper.

Suitable for freezing, before cooking (see Deep Freezing, page 15). Thaw on baking trays for 30 minutes, and bake at 225° C (435° F) for 8–9 minutes, or deep fry. They may be baked or fried in advance, and re-heated in the oven at 200° C (400° F) for 5–6 minutes.

## FILLINGS FOR PUFF PASTRY TURNOVERS

All the fillings for Shortcrust Turnovers (pages 143–4) are suitable for Puff Pastry Turnovers, and all recipes for Bouchées (pages 152–3). They are all suitable for freezing, and for preparing a day in advance, and refrigerating.

### Cheese Filling

*170 g (6 oz) processed gruyère*
*or bel paese cheese*

Cut into flat rectangles of a size to fit easily into the turnover.

### Cheese and Ham Filling

*90 g (3 oz) processed gruyère*          *90 g (3 oz) ham, minced or cut*
*or bel paese cheese*                           *in small pieces*

Cut the cheese as in previous recipe, and divide the ham and cheese between the turnovers.

### Ham and Tomato Filling

*110 g (4 oz) ham, minced or*          *60 g (2 oz) onion, finely*
*cut in small pieces*                          *chopped*
*60 g (2 oz) tomatoes, skinned*       *2 tablespoons oil*
*and de-seeded, chopped*               *salt and black pepper*

Sauté the onions in the oil for 5–10 minutes or till soft. Add the tomatoes and cook until most of the juice has boiled away. Add the ham, and season.

### Sardine Filling

*125 g (4½ oz) sardine*          *2 tablespoons cream*
*2 teaspoons lemon juice*

Mash the sardines and mix with the lemon juice and cream.

## Salmon or Tunafish Puffs

Puff pastry dough (page 176) using:

*90 g (3 oz) plain flour*          *150 g (5½ oz) cooked salmon,*
*good pinch salt*                   *or tunafish*
*90 g (3 oz) very cold margarine*  *2 teaspoons lemon juice*
*few drops lemon juice*            *2 tablespoons cream*
*3 tablespoons very cold water*    *salt and black pepper*

Roll the dough to just over 38 cm by 30 cm (15 in by 12 in). Divide this
into 4 pieces, each 38 cm by 7½ cm (15 in by 3 in) long. Cut each
piece into 9 short strips, 7½ cm (3 in) long. Mash the fish with the
lemon juice and cream, season, and place a little near one end of
each strip. Damp the edges of one end, and bring the other end over,
and seal firmly. Paint with a mixture of egg and 2 teaspoons water, if
wished. Bake at 225° C (435° F) for 7–8 minutes, or deep fry at 200° C
(400° F). There is no point in painting with egg and water if frying.

Suitable for freezing or preparing in advance (page 15).

## Puff Pastry Pinwheels

Puff pastry dough (page 176) using the same quantities as in the
previous recipe plus:
*various fillings*

Roll the dough to just over 30 cm by 26 cm (12 in by 10 in) and
continue as for Shortcrust Pinwheels (pages 141–2), using the same
fillings.

Suitable for freezing and for preparing in advance as for Shortcrust
Pinwheels.

## Cheese Horseshoes

Puff pastry dough (page 176) using:
*170 g (6 oz) plain flour*          *1 small egg, lightly beaten*
*¼ teaspoon salt*                   *3½ teaspoons tomato ketchup*
*170 g (6 oz) very cold margarine*  *30 g (1 oz) onion, chopped finely*
*1 teaspoon lemon juice*            *30 g (1 oz) butter or margarine*
*6 tablespoons very cold water*     *1 small egg mixed with 2*
*140 g (5 oz) bel paese or*          *teaspoons water for sealing*
*processed gruyère cheese*          *and browning*

Divide the dough into 3. Roll each piece to just over 26 cm by 19 cm
(10 in by 7½ in). Cut into 5 cm (2½ in) squares. Mix the beaten egg
with the grated cheese until well blended. Add the tomato ketchup.
Sauté the onion for 5–10 minutes, or till soft, in the butter or mar-

garine, and add to the mixture. Place a teaspoonful in the centre of each square, and damp the edges with the egg and water mixture. Lift one corner and cover the filling, and then roll it to the opposite corner. Bring the pointed sides to meet at the front and form a circle. Press them together to make them stick. (These will gradually open out while cooking, to form a crescent.) Paint with the remaining egg and water mixture. Bake for 18–20 minutes at 200°C (400°F).

Suitable for freezing after cooking (see Deep Freezing, page 15). Thaw on baking trays for 30 minutes and re-heat for 7–8 minutes at 200°C (400°F). May also be prepared completely in advance and re-heated for 8–9 minutes at 200°C (400°F).

# 4(d). Choux Pastries

**EACH RECIPE IS FOR 36 PASTRIES**

Hot or cold          **Savoury Éclairs**

*half quantity choux pastry*        *1 small egg mixed with 1*
  *dough (page 176)*                *teaspoon water*

1. *To make small, round savoury éclairs*:
Make the dough using the recipe on page 176, half quantities. With a forcing bag, pipe small rounds, about 2 cm (less than 1 in) in diameter, on a baking tray. If you have no forcing bag, drop small teaspoonsful, making them as round as possible. Flatten the tops very slightly, with a pastry brush, or small house-painting brush, dipped in a mixture of egg and water, and bake at 210°C (425°F) for 18–20 minutes.

Just before the éclairs are ready, take them out of the oven, and slit them with the point of a very sharp knife. Replace them in the oven for 1–2 minutes. They should be golden brown, and feel slightly crisp.

2. *To make long éclairs*:
Pipe the mixture into lines 4½ cm (1¾ in) long. There is no need to flatten them, but they should be painted with the egg and water mixture. Bake at 210°C (425°F) for 12–14 minutes.

Éclairs can be kept warm in a low oven for several minutes without taking harm. When required, take out, slice off the tops, and fill with any of the following fillings. The top can either be replaced, or left off to show the filling inside. If left off, there is no need to paint with the egg and water. (To keep any unused dough, see Choux Pastry Dough (page 176).

Suitable for freezing. To re-heat, thaw for 20 minutes and bake at 200°C (400°F) for 3–4 minutes. May be prepared in advance, and stored in an airtight container for 2–3 days, and re-heated.


## FILLINGS FOR ÉCLAIRS

The cold fillings may all be prepared in advance, but the éclairs should not be filled more than a few hours before use.


Hot      **Cheese Filling**

45 g (1½oz) butter or margarine
45 g (1½oz) flour
3 dl (½ pint) milk
½ level teaspoon salt

pinch cayenne pepper
1 egg yolk
170 g (6 oz) gruyère or emmenthal cheese
30 g (1 oz) parmesan cheese

Make a white sauce with the butter, flour, milk and seasonings (page 68). Remove from the heat. Add the egg yolk, and mix well into the sauce, and mix in the cheese, grated. Do not re-boil. When cooler, spoon into the empty éclairs, and sprinkle with parmesan. Replace tops, if wished. Return to the oven and re-heat at 200°C (400°F) for 4–5 minutes.

The separate items, the éclairs and the sauce, may be frozen, but should not be frozen once the éclairs are filled. They may be prepared a few hours in advance, and re-heated at 200°C (400°F) for 7–8 minutes.


Cold      **Sardine, Salmon or Tuna Filling**

110 g (4 oz) sardine, mashed, or salmon, or tunafish
2 teaspoons lemon juice

2 teaspoons chopped parsley
2 tablespoons cream
salt and black pepper

Mix all ingredients, till smooth. Fill the éclair cases.


Cold      **Sour Cream and Caviare Filling**

4 tablespoons thick sour cream

75 g (2½oz) lumpfish caviare

Whip the sour cream till very thick, and fill the éclair cases. Sprinkle the caviare on top. Do not replace the tops.

Cold **Prawn Mayonnaise Filling**

3½ tablespoons thick Paprika
  Mayonnaise (page 70) or
  Curry Mayonnaise (page 70)

140 g (5 oz) prawns, very finely
  chopped, or substitute some
  very finely chopped celery
  for some of the prawns

Mix the ingredients together and fill the éclair cases.

Cold **Chicken and Chilli Filling**

110 g (4 oz) minced chicken,
  or turkey, or ham
3 tablespoons Chilli Sauce
  (page 67)

3 tablespoons thick cream
a little finely chopped celery,
  or pineapple, if wished

Mix all ingredients together and fill the éclair cases.

Hot or cold **Cheese Puffs**

double quantities choux
  pastry dough (page 176)
60 g (2 oz) gruyère or
  emmenthal cheese

45 g (1½ oz) parmesan cheese,
  or finely grated almonds
1 small egg mixed with 2
  teaspoons water

Make the dough for choux pastry as described on page 176. Beat the
gruyère or emmenthal, finely grated, into the choux dough, and
correct seasoning if necessary. Pipe or place teaspoonsful on a
baking tray, paint with the egg and water mixture, and sprinkle with
the parmesan or almonds. Bake at 210° C (425° F) for 14 minutes. Slit
with the point of a very sharp knife just before they are ready, and
replace in oven for a further 1–2 minutes. Do not remove the tops, or
fill, as they need no filling. Serve hot or cold.

Suitable for freezing, and for preparing in advance as for éclairs.

Hot **Cheese and Ham Puffs**

30 g (1 oz) butter
4 tablespoons water
60 g (2 oz) plain flour
2 medium eggs, lightly beaten
90 g (3 oz) gruyère or
  emmenthal cheese, or 45 g
  (1½ oz) cheddar

45 g (1½ oz) ham, finely
  chopped or minced
10 g (⅓ oz) onion, very finely
  chopped

For the dressing:
*30 g (1 oz) plain flour*
*1 small egg mixed with 1*
  *teaspoon water*

*90 g (3 oz) fresh white*
  *breadcrumbs*

1. Make the choux dough by the method described on page 176, but using the above quantities. Beat in the cheese, grated finely, and the ham and onion. When cool, roll into balls the size of small marbles, cover with flour, egg and water mixture and breadcrumbs.

2. Either deep fry at 200°C (400°F) till golden brown, or bake at the same temperature for 18 minutes. Drain on absorbent paper before serving.

Suitable for freezing after completing 1. To cook, thaw for 30 minutes and continue with 2. Or after 2, and re-heat by baking for 5–6 minutes at 200°C (400°F). May be prepared in advance to the end of 1. Continue with 2. Or to the end of 2. Re-heat in the oven for 5–6 minutes at 200°C (400°F).

# 4(e). Pizza Pastries and Savoury Scones

**EACH RECIPE MAKES 36 UNLESS OTHERWISE STATED**

Hot      **Baby Pizzas**

For the dough:
*170 g (6 oz) plain flour*
*1½ level teaspoons salt*
*1½ level teaspoons sugar*
*1½ level teaspoons dried yeast*
*1 dl (⅙ pint) warm milk*
*1 small egg*
*45 g (1½ oz) butter or margarine*

For the basic filling:
*60 g (2 oz) onion, finely chopped*
*1½ tablespoons olive oil*
*450 g (16 oz) tomatoes, skinned and chopped, or a large can, drained, to give approx. 335 g (12 oz)*
*1½ teaspoons fresh basil, thyme or oregano, or 1 teaspoon if dried*
*1 medium clove garlic, crushed*
*salt*

Alternative additions to basic filling:
A. *110 g (4 oz) gruyère or bel paese cheese, in small, thin slices with 12 anchovies, sliced thinly or chopped*
B. *110 g (4 oz) mushrooms, chopped finely or sliced, sautéed in 1 tablespoon olive oil*
C. *90 g (3 oz) salami, finely sliced and quartered, allowing 2 quarters per pizza*
D. *110 g (4 oz) clams (or vongoles) mixed with ½ tablespoon olive oil*
E. *90 g (3 oz) tunafish, broken into small pieces, topped with 90 g (3 oz) black olives stoned and chopped*
F. *90 g (3 oz) red and/or green sweet peppers, sliced and chopped, mixed with 1 tablespoon olive oil*
G. *110 g (4 oz) shrimps or peeled prawns, chopped or left whole*

H. *110 g (4 oz) bacon, finely chopped, and pre-fried, or 60 g (2 oz) bacon and 60 g (2 oz) mushrooms*

I. *90 g (3 oz) Frankfurter sausages, cut into thin rounds, allowing 3 rounds per pizza*

J. *90 g (3 oz) chopped ham*

1. Dissolve the sugar in the warm milk, sprinkle the dried yeast over the milk, stir once, and leave for 10 minutes, or until frothy. Sieve the flour and salt together into a warm basin. Beat the egg lightly, and add the egg, the milk, sugar and yeast mixture to the flour, mixing carefully to make a soft dough. Sprinkle on a little extra flour, shape the dough into a ball, and remove from the bowl onto a lightly floured surface. Soften the butter, or margarine, place on top of the dough, and knead in gently. When absorbed, replace the dough in the bowl, cover and leave in a warm place for at least 1 hour, or until well risen.

2. While it is rising, make the filling. Heat the olive oil in a pan, add the onion and cook very gently, for about 10 minutes, until soft. Add the tomatoes, herbs, garlic and seasonings, and simmer for a further 15 minutes, or until well reduced and thick. (The amount of salt needed depends largely on the saltiness of the other ingredients, e.g. the cheese, anchovies, olives, etc.)

3. Divide the dough in half, for easier handling, and roll into a long sausage 45 cm (18 in) long. Slice across the sausage at 2½ cm (1 in) intervals, to make 18 pieces. Roll these into little balls, and press gently with the knuckles, to flatten. Place on an oiled baking tray.

4. Spread each baby pizza with a well-filled teaspoon of filling, and add whichever addition you have selected.

5. Bake at 200° C (400° F) for 14 minutes. Serve hot.

Suitable for freezing after 4. The pizza must first be frozen uncovered, and when firm packed into containers. To re-heat, place the frozen pizzas on a baking tray for 30 minutes to thaw, then bake at 200° C (400° F) for 7–8 minutes.

Hot             **False Pizzas**          Makes 36 or 48
(Baby Pizzas using a Scone Mixture Base)

For the scone dough:
335 g (12 oz) plain flour
6 level teaspoons baking
  powder, or 1½ level
  teaspoons cream of tartar
  and ¾ level teaspoon
  bicarbonate of soda
½ level teaspoon salt

90 g (3 oz) margarine
2¼ dl (1½ gills) milk

For the basic filling:
*See previous recipe*

For alternative additions:
*See previous recipe*

1. Sift the flour and salt, with either the baking powder, or the cream of tartar and bicarbonate of soda, into a bowl, and rub in the margarine with fingertips till the mixture resembles fine breadcrumbs. Stir in the milk a little at a time, until it forms a very soft dough. Turn it onto a well-floured board, and knead gently till it forms a smooth ball. Divide it into three for easier handling.
2. Roll each piece to approximately 20 cm by 15 cm (8 in by 6 in) and cut 12 circles from each, with a 5 cm (2 in) cutter.
3. Place a well-filled teaspoonful of basic filling on each, and add whichever additions you have selected.
4. Bake at 240°C (460°F) for 8 minutes. Serve hot.

Suitable for freezing after 3 (see previous recipe). They may also be frozen after 4, and re-heated at 170°C (340°F) for 7–8 minutes. May be prepared in advance to the end of 3. Continue with 4.

Hot          **Curry-flavoured Scones**

For the dough:
*half the quantity of scone dough (page 163)*
*1–2 teaspoons curry powder*
*45 g (1½ oz) cheddar cheese, finely grated*

For the filling:
A. *scrambled eggs (page 105) using 4 large eggs, and 2 teaspoons parsley*
B. *for other suggestions, see Hot Canapés section (pages 102–9)*

1. As for False Pizzas (page 163), adding the curry powder and grated cheese after rubbing in the margarine, but do not divide the dough into three.
2. Roll the dough to approximately 30 cm by 15 cm (12 in by 6 in). Cut 18 circles with a 5 cm (2 in) cutter.
3. Bake at 240°C (460°F) for 9 minutes.
4. Split in half and use each half as a base. Place a little filling on each, sprinkle with chopped parsley, and serve hot.

Suitable for freezing after completing 3. To re-heat, thaw for 30 minutes, and bake at 240°C (460°F) for 5 minutes. Continue with 4.

Hot          **Cheese Scones**

For the dough:
*half the quantity of scone dough (page 163)*
*60–110 g (2–4 oz) cheddar cheese, finely grated*
*½ level teaspoon dry mustard*
*pinch cayenne pepper*

For the filling:
*thin slices of cheese, with parsley, chopped ham, chopped tomato or chutney*

1. As for False Pizzas (page 163), adding the grated cheese, cayenne and dry mustard after rubbing in the margarine, but do not divide into three.

2, 3 and 4. As for Curry-flavoured Scones (page 164), but replace the scones in the oven after filling, to allow the cheese to melt. Sprinkle with parsley. Serve hot.

Suitable for freezing, and for preparing in advance, as for Curry-flavoured Scones.

Hot          **Cheese Scone Rolls**

For the dough:
*one-quarter of the quantity of
  scone dough (page 163)*
*45 g (1½ oz) cheddar cheese,
  finely grated*
*30 g (1 oz) bacon, pre-fried
  and finely chopped*
*½ egg, lightly beaten*
*pinch cayenne*

For the rolls:
*60 g (2 oz) plain flour*
*1 small egg mixed with 1
  teaspoon water*
*60 g (2 oz) parmesan cheese*
*45 g (1½ oz) butter*

1. As for False Pizzas (page 163), adding the grated cheese, bacon and cayenne after rubbing in the margarine, but do not divide into 3.

2. Take pieces of dough the size of a walnut and roll into sausage shapes. Roll them in the flour, dip in the egg and water mixture, and roll in the parmesan.

3. Bake at 225° C (430° F) for 9 minutes.

4. Remove from the oven, and make a small slit along the top of each roll and insert a thin piece of butter. Serve hot at once, while the butter is melting.

Suitable for freezing after completing 2. To cook, thaw for 30 minutes and continue from 3. May be prepared in advance to the end of 2. Continue with 3 and 4.

# 4(f). Unusual Pastries

**EACH RECIPE IS FOR 36 PASTRIES**

Hot
## Empanadas
### (Minced Meat enclosed in a Special Pastry)

For the pastry:
*225 g (8 oz) plain flour*
*1 level teaspoon salt*
*30 g (1 oz) butter or lard*

*1 egg, beaten lightly*
*approximately 2 tablespoons cold water*

For the filling:
*60 g (2 oz) onion, finely chopped*
*4 tablespoons oil*
*170 g (6 oz) cooked meat, or a meat which will cook very quickly, such as chicken breast or pork fillet, finely minced*

*2 teaspoons flour*
*8 tablespoons stock*
*4 well-rounded teaspoons Chilli Sauce (page 67)*

1. Mix the flour and salt and sieve into a large bowl. Mix in the fat with the thumbs and fingertips till it resembles fine breadcrumbs. Mix in the egg and water to form a soft dough. Rest for 1 hour in the refrigerator. Divide the dough into 2. Roll out very thinly indeed, to just over 26 cm (10 in) square each. With a 4 cm (1½ in) fluted cutter, mark 36 circles on one square, but do not cut through. Lay a spoonful of filling in the centre of each circle. Lay the second piece of dough over the first, allowing enough dough to be able to press down between the humps of filling, and leaving no airgaps. Press down between the humps with the side of the hand, to seal. Cut with the cutter, and check seals again. To make the filling, sauté the onion in the oil, add the flour and stir, add the stock, and when thick mix with the other ingredients.
2. Deep fry at 200° C (400° F) till golden brown.

Suitable for freezing after completing 1 (see Deep Freezing, page 15). Thaw on baking trays and continue with 2. Not suitable for preparing in advance.

Hot                 **Wontons**
(Chinese Savoury Pies)

For the pastry:
*use as for Empanadas in the previous recipe*

For the filling:
*use the recipe for Chicken and Mushroom in Ginger (page 129), slightly increasing the spices*

Method as for Empanadas, and may similarly be frozen.

Hot                 **Chinese Spring Rolls**

For the pastry:
*400 g (14 oz) plain flour*
*1 teaspoon salt*

*just over 3 dl (½ pint) warm water*

For the filling:
*120 g (4¼ oz) raw pork, minced*
*120 g (4¼ oz) shelled prawns, or shrimps, chopped*
*120 g (4¼ oz) bean sprouts*
*120 g (4¼ oz) mushrooms, chopped*
*30 g (1 oz) spring onions, or shallots, or onion, chopped*

*50 g (just under 2 oz) crystallized ginger, finely chopped*
*½ teaspoon salt*
*black pepper*
*2 tablespoons sake or dry sherry*

1. Mix the flour and salt and sieve into a bowl. Gradually add the warm water while stirring, until a soft dough is made. Rest in the refrigerator for 1 hour. Divide the dough into 2 and roll each piece very thinly to 38 cm by 19 cm (15 in by 7½ in). Marinate all ingredients for the filling in the sake or sherry, while the pastry is resting. Cut the dough into 36 squares of 6 cm (2½ in) and damp with a little water. Place a little of the filling on each. Fold one corner over the filling, fold one side corner over, then the other, and then roll firmly to the furthest corner. Make sure that the end has sealed. This is quite a difficult recipe, and if preferred the rolls can be made a little larger, which makes it easier.
2. Deep fry at 200°C (400°F).

Suitable for freezing after completing 1 (see Deep Freezing, page 15). Thaw on baking trays for 30 minutes and continue with 2. May be prepared on the same day, and refrigerated, covered in foil to prevent drying out.

Hot

## Fritelle Pastry
(Italian Pastry)

For the pastry:
*110 g (4 oz) plain flour*
*30 g (1 oz) butter*
*¼ teaspoon salt*
*1 tablespoon boiling water*

For the filling:
*90 g (3 oz) bel paese cheese,*
*cut into 36 small squares*

1. Mix the flour with the salt, and mix in the butter, as in the previous recipe. Add the water and mix quickly to a dough. Divide the dough in 2, and roll each piece out to just over 30 cm (12 in) square. This makes it very thin indeed. Mark one piece into 36 squares (6 × 6) but do not cut through, and cut off any untidy edges. Place a piece of cheese in the centre of each square. Lay the other piece of dough on top, and press firmly between the humps with the side of the hand, leaving no airgaps between the cheese and the dough. This must be done very quickly as the dough dries out very soon, and splits. Cut between the humps, and check that all seams are sealed.
2. Deep fry for 1 minute, turning the pastries over after 30 seconds.

Suitable for freezing (see Deep Freezing, page 15). Thaw on baking trays for 20 minutes and continue with 2. Not suitable for preparing in advance.

## FILLINGS FOR FRITELLE PASTRIES

### Veal and Ham Filling

*110 g (4 oz) lean veal, or lamb,*
*cooked*
*30 g (1 oz) ham, or lean bacon,*
*fried*

*1 dessertspoon stock*
*1 egg yolk*
*30 g (1 oz) parmesan, grated*
*salt and black pepper*

Mince the meat and ham or bacon together very finely, and add the parmesan, stock and egg yolk. If possible, blend in an electric blender. Season.

### Cheese Filling

*60 g (2 oz) parmesan cheese,*
*grated*
*90 g (3 oz) bel paese, or*
*processed gruyère, grated*

*1 large egg, lightly beaten*
*1 tablespoon milk*
*black pepper*
*pinch fresh herbs if available*

Blend all the ingredients together, if possible in an electric blender.

### Spicy Filling

*125 g (4½ oz) raw beef,*
*minced*
*½ clove garlic, crushed*
*½ teaspoon chopped parsley*
*45 g (1½ oz) onion, chopped*
*2 tablespoons oil*

*2 tablespoons stock*
*30 g (1 oz) tomato paste*
*2 level teaspoons allspice, or*
*1 level teaspoon cumin or*
*cinnamon*
*salt and black pepper*

Brown the beef in the oil, then add the onion and stock and simmer 30 minutes, adding more stock if necessary (but finally allowing it to evaporate to an almost solid sauce). Add the garlic, parsley, tomato paste and allspice, and simmer till thick enough. Season. Allow to cool before placing on the dough.

### Chicken Liver Filling

*110 g (4 oz) chicken livers,*
*chopped*
*60 g (2 oz) butter*

*45 g (1½ oz) bacon, chopped*
*4 tablespoons stock*
*1 small egg yolk*

Sauté the bacon, add the butter and chicken livers and cook for 3–4 minutes. Add the stock and simmer a further 10 minutes until the stock has almost evaporated. Cool and stir in the egg yolk. Blend together in an electric blender, if possible. If no blender is available, press the mixture into a tight ball in the hand, and place in the centre of the square. The filling should be cold before placing on the dough.


Hot                              **Burek**
                              (Fila Pastries)

It is never worth while making Fila pastry at home, as it is a great deal of work, and far better can be bought at Greek or Turkish shops, ready to use. Fila pastry comes in very thin sheets. To make it thicker, if required, the sheets are held together by painting one sheet with melted butter, and laying a second sheet on top. It is very important not to expose the sheets to the air more than can be helped, as they dry out very quickly and start to crack. Always keep the roll of sheets covered unless actually using them. Fila pastries are made by cutting the sheets into strips, adding a filling and rolling them into various shapes. They are then deep fried, or painted with butter and baked at 200° C (400° F) for about 18 minutes.


A. *The simple roll*: Use double thickness Fila, with a layer of butter in between. Cut the sheet into 4 long strips. Lay the filling in the centre near one end. Bring the end over to cover the filling, and bring the sides over one at a time, so that the filling is enclosed on three sides. Then roll it over and over to the end of the sheets. Spread a little extra butter at the end, to seal.

B. *The triangle*: Use double thickness Fila, with a layer of butter in between, and cut the sheet into 4 long strips and brush again with butter. Lay the filling near one end and fold one corner of the strip of Fila over the filling to form a triangle over the filling. Now bend the area with the filling straight down the strip, so that you have a rectangular end again. Then, holding the triangle, bend it over its own base, diagonally across the strip; then bend it straight down the strip again making a rectangular end once more. Continue in this way until all the Fila is used up. Seal the end by tucking the last bit of the strip into the triangle.

C. *The square*: Use double thickness Fila, with a layer of butter in between. Fold exactly as for the simple roll, but instead of rolling it over and over, form a flat square with the back end and sides, and turn this over and over down the strip. Seal the end with a little extra butter.

D. *The cigar*: Use double thickness Fila, with a layer of butter in between. Cut the sheet in half, lengthwise. Lay the filling along 7 cm (3 in) of the narrow end. Fold the end over it, and bring the sides up over the ends, as with the simple roll. Roll the pastry over and over to the other end, forming a long, thin shape like a cigar.

E. *The pinwheel*: Use double thickness Fila, with a layer of butter in between, and cut the sheet in half lengthwise. Make a long, thin roll, as for the cigar, using slightly less filling, so that it is more pliable. Curl these round into pinwheels. Pack close together while baking, to prevent uncurling. Once cooked they will remain in shape.

F. *The pirog*: Use double thickness Fila, with a layer of butter in between. Paint the sheet again with more butter. Cut circles of either 5 cm (2 in) or 6 cm (2¼ in), lay the filling in the middle, and bring up the sides to form a pyramid (see Shortcrust Pastries, page 140). The 6 cm pirog will require almost twice as much filling as the 5 cm.

## FILLINGS FOR BUREK

### Meat Filling

Use the recipe for Spicy Filling (page 169).

### Gruyère and Spinach Filling

200 g (7 oz) frozen chopped
  spinach
30 g (1 oz) butter
110 g (4 oz) processed gruyère
  or bel paese cheese, grated

1 small egg
15 g (½ oz) chopped pine
  kernels, browned in a little
  butter, optional
salt and black pepper

Squeeze out as much water as possible from the spinach and then simmer in the butter until the rest has evaporated. Add the grated cheese, the egg, seasoning and pine if used. Cook very carefully to allow the egg and cheese to thicken, but do not boil.

### Feta Cheese and Herb Filling

170 g (6 oz) feta cheese,
  obtainable from Greek or
  Turkish shops

6 teaspoons chopped herbs,
  including parsley, mint,
  chives, etc.
1 small egg, lightly beaten
salt and black pepper

Mash the cheese with the egg and add the other ingredients. Season.

## Tunafish Filling

170 g (6 oz) tunafish with some       1 tablespoon oil
  of its oil                          1 small egg, lightly beaten
60 g (2 oz) onion, chopped            salt and black pepper

Mash the tunafish with the egg. Sauté the onion in the oil for 5–10
minutes or till soft. Mix with the tunafish, and season.

## Cheese Sauce Fillings

Use any of the variations of the Cheese Fillings for Éclairs (pages
159–60).

## Burek using Puff Pastry

For the pastry:
*Puff pastry dough (page 176) using*:
140 g (5 oz) plain flour              1 small teaspoon lemon juice
⅓ level teaspoon salt                 5 tablespoons very cold water
140 g (5 oz) very cold
  margarine

For the filling:
*use any of the recipes for Fila
  pastries in the previous
  recipe*

Divide the dough into 2 and roll each piece to just over 38 cm by
19 cm (15 in by 7½ in). Using a 6 cm (2¼ in) cutter, cut 18 circles from
each (6 × 3). Fill with the selected filling, damp the edges and bend
over to form the letter D, as in a turnover. Seal the edges. Either paint
with egg and water mixture and bake at 200° C (400° F) for 8–9
minutes; or deep fry. Or, from the same dough, cut 6 cm (2¼ in)
squares. Place filling to one side of centre, damp the edges and
bring one corner across to the opposite, to form a triangle. Seal the
edges. Bake or fry as above.

Suitable for freezing (a) before cooking (see Deep Freezing, page
15). Thaw on baking trays for 30 minutes and bake or fry as above. Or
(b) after cooking. Re-heat at 200° C (400° F) for 5–6 minutes. May be
prepared in advance earlier in the day, covered with foil, if
uncooked, and refrigerated, and cooked or re-heated as above.

Hot        ## Pirogs made with Puff Pastry

For the pastry:                       For the fillings:
*puff pastry dough (page 176)         *use any of the recipes for Fila
  using one-quarter of the              pastries (pages 171–2)*
  quantities given*

Roll the dough to just over 32 cm (12½ in) square and cut 36 circles with a 5 cm (2 in) cutter. Fill with the selected filling, and make into pyramids using the method described on page 171. Or, divide the dough in half and roll each piece to just over 38 cm by 18 cm (15 in by 7 in) and cut 18 squares at 6 cm (2¼ in) from each (6 × 3). Fill with the selected filling and make into four-sided burek, using the method described on page 170. Use half as much again of the filling.

Hot or cold            **Sambusak**
(Middle Eastern pastries)

For the pastry:
*110 g (4 oz) plain flour*
*2 tablespoons oil*
*30 g (1 oz) butter*
*2 tablespoons warm water*
*¼ teaspoon salt*

Fillings:
*these should always be moist,*
*as the pastry is very 'short',*
*that is, dry and powdery*

Warm the oil and butter until the butter has melted, then add the water and salt, and pour into a bowl containing the flour. Stir till quite smooth. Remove with well-floured hands, and divide into 2. Roll each half to just over 38 cm by 18 cm (15 in by 7 in). Using the 6 cm (2¼ in) cutter cut 18 circles from each (6 × 3). Fill with the selected filling by placing a teaspoonful in the centre. Damp the edges. Bring both sides up to meet over the filling, and press firmly together to seal. (It should now look like a Cornish pasty.) Paint with egg and water mixture, if wished. Bake at 200° C (400° F) for 10–12 minutes, or deep fry.

Sambusak are suitable for freezing (a) before cooking (see Deep Freezing, page 15). Thaw on baking trays for 30 minutes and paint with egg and water mixture, and bake at 200° C (400° F) for 10–12 minutes, or deep fry. Or (b) after cooking. Thaw and re-heat at 200° C (400° F) for 7–8 minutes.

## FILLINGS FOR SAMBUSAK

### Cheese Filling

*60 g (2 oz) gruyère, grated*      *1 small egg, lightly beaten*
*60 g (2 oz) parmesan, grated*    *salt and black pepper*

Mix the cheese and blend with the egg. Season.

## Other Fillings

Use any of the recipes for Fila Pastries (171–2) or the recipe for Spicy
Filling (page 169).

# 4(g). Pastry Recipes

## Shortcrust Pastry    Makes 450 g (1 lb)

255 g (9 oz) plain flour
170 g (6 oz) very cold
  margarine

2 tablespoons very cold water
½ teaspoon salt

Sieve the flour into a large bowl. Cut the margarine into small pieces, and add to the flour. With the thumbs and fingertips, pick up the pieces of margarine, and rub them through the flour, until they have all amalgamated with the flour to form the consistency of bread-crumbs. Add the salt, and the water, mixing with a knife. When it is damp enough it will start to bind together. When it forms one large ball, place in a floured polythene bag, and leave to rest in a cool place, preferably a refrigerator, for at least 30 minutes. Place on a floured board, and roll to the size required.

To freeze, leave in the ball, in the polythene bag, and tie securely, or roll out, fold into a convenient shape, and then place in the bag. The advantage of rolling first is that it will then take less time to thaw when needed.

## Cheese Shortcrust Pastry    Makes 450 g (1 lb) approx.

255 g (9 oz) plain flour
125 g (4½ oz) very cold butter
  or margarine
125 g (4½ oz) cheese (cheddar
  or cheddar with a little
  parmesan)

1 level teaspoon salt
good pinch cayenne pepper
⅓ teaspoon dry mustard
1 large egg yolk mixed with 1
  or more tablespoons very
  cold water

Sift together the flour, salt, cayenne pepper and dry mustard into a large bowl. Mix in the butter or margarine, as for shortcrust. Add the cheese, very finely grated, and the egg and water mix. If using a machine, 1 tablespoon water should be enough, but if mixing by hand you will probably require more. Continue exactly as for shortcrust, resting the pastry before use. It may similarly be frozen.

If a particularly 'short' pastry is required, i.e. even lighter and more crumbly, as for example for cheese straws or biscuits, increase the quantity of butter or margarine, while keeping the rest of the quantities the same.

## Puff Pastry  Makes 900 g (2 lb)

Home-made pastry, using 450 g (1 lb) flour is the equivalent to bought, ready-made pastry weighing 900 g (2 lb). In all recipes in this book, ready-made pastry can be used in place of home-made; if the recipe specifies 225 g (8 oz) flour, use ready-made weighing 450 g (1 lb).

*450 g (1 lb) plain flour*
*1 level teaspoon salt*
*450 g (1 lb) butter or margarine*

*2 teaspoons lemon juice*
*just under 3 dl (½ pint) very*
 *cold water*

Sift the flour and salt into a large bowl. Divide the butter into 4. Rub one quarter of the butter into the flour, as in shortcrust, then add the water and lemon juice, and form a dough, using a knife. Turn onto a floured board and knead until smooth. Place in a polythene bag, in a cold place, preferably the refrigerator for 30 minutes. Form the remaining butter into a slab 13 cm (5 in) square on a floured board. Roll the dough to 28 cm by 15 cm (11 in by 6 in). Place the butter at one end, leaving a narrow border free at the end and round the sides. Fold the other half of the dough over the butter end, and press the edges together to seal them firmly. Turn the dough so that the fold is on the left-hand side. Roll the dough away from you, with the rolling pin, till it measures 30 cm by 15 cm (12 in by 6 in). Fold the bottom third, i.e. the third nearest you, upwards, and the top third, furthest away, towards you to cover it. Press the edges firmly together to seal again. Turn the dough so as to have the fold on the left-hand side again. Roll as before to 30 cm by 15 cm (12 in by 6 in) and fold as before, and seal. Place in a polythene bag in the refrigerator for 1 hour. Roll 4 more times, exactly as before, resting the dough 10–15 minutes between each rolling, in the refrigerator. Give it a final rest of 30 minutes. Roll to the size required, and use.

Puff pastry can be frozen, or it will keep in the refrigerator for 3–4 days.

## Choux Pastry  Makes 450 g (1 lb)

*1½ dl (¼ pint) water*
*45 g (1½ oz) butter, in small*
 *pieces*
*½ teaspoon salt*

*good pinch black pepper*
*60 g (2 oz) plain flour*
*2 medium eggs*

Bring the water to the boil in a small pan with the butter and seasonings. The butter should have melted just as the water comes to the boil. Add the flour all at once, and beat with a wooden spoon till blended. Continue beating till the mixture leaves the sides of the pan, forming one large ball – this should only take one minute. Remove from the heat, make a depression in the dough, and break in 1 egg. Beat at once until it has completely amalgamated with the dough. Add the second egg, and repeat. The dough is now ready for use, and should be used while still warm.

Keep any unused dough covered with foil. It can be re-used after cooling, by re-warming in a bowl over hot water, or by placing in a bowl already warmed, and by beating gently to absorb the heat. It can be refrigerated for 2–3 days.

Choux dough can be frozen. Re-warm carefully, using the above method.

# 5

# ON RUNNING A SMALL CATERING BUSINESS

This book was written for people entertaining in their own homes, but it may also be of use to those who are thinking of running a small catering business. Many of the recipes included are particularly suitable for the home cook to make in quantity in her own kitchen.

Although there is a great deal to be said on the subject which is beyond the scope of this book, I am, in this chapter, offering a few suggestions gathered from my own experience which may help you to decide whether or not to try running your own business, and, if so, how to obtain the maximum enjoyment and profit from it.

## Organization

First, there are a number of questions you must ask yourself about how you are going to run the business. Are you going to do it entirely alone? Or with some kind of help? Or will you take one or more partners?

If you decide you would like to work alone, then there are a number of things you must think about. What is going to happen when you are ill, or if you want a holiday? Remember that one of the most important things about any kind of service is its reliability. Customers expect you to be there when they need you, and so you will have to find some way of providing for this contingency.

If you are on holiday perhaps it would be worth having a recording system installed on your telephone. Or maybe you could get the help of a friend. But be certain that she knows how to do everything exactly as you did. She may have a recipe for a pâté which she considers superior to yours, and, indeed, it may be. But the customer who has already tried yours, and has given a repeat order, will expect to get the same again. And make certain she doesn't change the sizes. Reducing them will annoy those who have ordered them before, and increasing them means that it will be difficult for you to reduce them again.

If you decide to do it alone, but with a certain amount of help, there are several different kinds of help to be considered. Will you want someone full-time, or only part-time? This could reduce the problem of sickness or holidays, but might necessitate paying them when they weren't needed. Will you employ someone by the hour? There are usually plenty of housewives only too willing to do a few hours a week, even very irregularly, either by helping you to prepare the food, or perhaps delivering it. Or do you know anyone with a particular flair for a certain kind of food – pastry, for example? She could supply you with her speciality when you need it.

Or will you work in partnership with a friend? Do you know anyone well enough to be sure that you can work together happily? How much time can she give, and how much can you? Will you both take the orders, or only one? And what about sharing the costs? If you are working from your own kitchen it is extremely difficult to separate the costs of the food used for the business from those used for your own consumption, but you will have to know to be able to charge up your expenses.

The most important thing in a partnership is to have absolutely clear agreements from the very start; in fact, it is disastrous not to.

How will you fix your prices? They will have to depend as much on supply and demand as on your costs. Get hold of the lists of any competitors, and see what their charges are; work out your own costs and see how they compare. You should be able to charge less than a big company with high overheads, even though their turnover may be far higher.

Keep in mind that time is money, whether it is that of your paid staff, or your own. An item using cheap ingredients may take a long time to prepare, and will therefore cost you a lot to produce though no one will be prepared to pay very much for it. On the other hand, smoked salmon or prawns, for example, may take very little time to prepare, and can be charged at a high price, making a substantial profit, despite the high cost of the ingredients. After all, if you take twice as long, you can only do half as many orders.

Some customers may prefer to collect their orders themselves, but the vast majority will want them to be delivered. Will you include delivery in your prices, or make a special charge? And how far are you prepared to drive?

Will you hire out glasses and dishes? A few customers may give you an order only on condition that you supply them. It is almost certainly worth while investing in them, if there seems to be a demand, as they will soon pay for themselves, and start to make a profit, even at quite a small charge, and breakages can be charged at full price. Will you collect them next day, or will you expect the customer to return them? And will you expect them to be washed? And will you ask for a deposit?

Will you provide staff to serve the drinks, hand round the food, or help in the customer's kitchen? Will you be prepared to go yourself, if asked? A lot of young people are very pleased to do this, but you must make sure that they look clean and tidy, and are dressed suitably for each particular occasion. They must know exactly how to behave, and be relied upon not to drink behind the scenes!

For some occasions, trained and uniformed barmen or waiters are required. The managers of local hotels or restaurants will sometimes cooperate by allowing you to employ those of their staff who are off-duty on a particular night, if the waiters themselves are willing, and they usually are.

And will you be expecting cash on delivery, or will you send out accounts?

How much notice will you require, and are you willing to discuss other ideas, or will you stick rigidly to what is shown on your lists?

## The Brochure

Once you have made up your mind on all these points, write your brochure. State the items you are prepared to offer, their price, your terms of business, and any other information you feel is relevant. Print it at whatever cost you can afford, remembering that presentation is tremendously important. No one will buy if the brochure looks like the work of an amateur. They can do things in an amateurish way themselves. What they are looking for is a professional.

A single sheet of paper is the cheapest, but this can be torn or lost far more easily than a small booklet, which will pay for itself in the end.

Date it, or number it, so that if you later want to produce a new list you can check that the customer is ordering from the latest edition.

## Public Relations

How will you let people know that you are now in business?

You can advertise in the local press, or in the church magazine, but this costs money.

The best way is to try to contact *directly* those to whom you feel your service will be of interest. These include any individuals who you know do a lot of entertaining, especially business entertaining, so send them a brochure. If your town is large enough there may be consulates, or small embassies who give a lot of parties but are not big enough to employ a regular staff. There are bound to be women's clubs, and business men's clubs. Write to the secretaries and send them a few copies, and ask them if they would be interested in receiving more for distribution among their members, or for displaying at their next meetings.

You could offer your firm's services as raffle prizes at local dances and charity fêtes, giving a maximum price.

The results may be slow to start with, but once you have catered for one or two parties, provided the quality of the food, the standard of service and the value are all good, the ball will soon start rolling. People are surprisingly willing to admit that they have employed caterers, and to hand on the name to those interested.

## Delivery

How will you transport your goods? The car or van used for delivery should have a large flat area, so that the trays with the savouries are never tilted. The trays should have sides high enough to come above the height of the savouries they contain, so that they can be stacked if necessary, criss-crossed, above each other.

Some shops are willing to give you the cardboard trays that have held beer or tinned foods, and these are ideal as they can be left behind at the customer's house if asked for. Or they can be made quite easily from wood. Check the dimensions of the area available in the car before starting to make them.

Everything must be covered, not only for reasons of cleanliness but also to prevent drying out. Aluminium foil is the best.

Don't forget that reliability of delivery is one of the most important parts of your service. No one will employ you again if you let them down. So what will you do on the occasions when your car isn't available, or if it refuses to start? Maybe you can arrange with a friendly neighbour to help you in an emergency, or take a taxi, though this could be very expensive.

The vital point is that you must arrive at the promised time. If you are one minute late your customers will have started to worry that you have forgotten, and the whole point of your service is that you are not only removing some of the work of entertaining, but some of the worry also. Be absolutely certain of the route, and, if necessary, make a practice run.

## Deep Freezing

How can you use the time between orders profitably? You can make a large supply of the savouries which appear to be the most popular, and freeze them. They should be clearly labelled with the type of contents, the quantity, date, and full instructions for thawing and cooking if necessary. You will find among your regular customers that there are some who will ring you up at the last moment to say they have unexpected guests, and what could you make at short notice? If you have time there and then, well and good, but if you are in the middle of another order, you might otherwise have to refuse a customer when she is particularly in need.

And customers may also ask you for supplies for their own freezers. This is a very profitable service, because it can also be done between orders, when you have time.

## Finally

Be adaptable, but don't agree to do the impossible just to get an order. And don't be tempted to do the first party at a loss, to show the marvellous value you offer. Those who know what you charged will expect you to do the same for them, at the same price.

On the other hand, give good value for money. Put in a few extra savouries, in case they are damaged in transit, and tell your customer that you have done so, so she won't be annoyed if one or two are damaged.

Remember always that you are offering a service, and not just food. You must realize that your customer is often nervous, especially the first time she employs you, and understandably so. She wants her party to be a success, and a large part of that success depends on someone about whom she knows very little.

From the moment she contacts you to discuss the possibility of placing an order with you, you must show her that as far as it is within your power her worries are now at an end. You must impress upon her not only your ability to produce good food, beautifully presented, but also your reliability.

Ring her the evening before, or on the morning of the party, and tell her that everything is in order and you will be there at the arranged time. And on the morning after the party ring again to ask how it went, and see if she was satisfied. It takes courage to do this, but it makes a wonderful impression that you care, and if she's going to complain, far better that she complains to you personally than that she should complain about you to all her friends. And then you have the opportunity to put things right with her.

Above all, you must have complete faith in yourself, and in your own ability, and, if you have, this will come across. You will then be performing not only a marvellous service for your customers but you will be ensuring repeat orders for yourself.

# INDEX

tunafish and black olives, 162
Pork
  Chinese meatballs, 42
  filling for open sandwiches, 87
  and game pâté, 92
  meatballs, 40
  pinwheels, 81
  tunnel rolls, 82
Potato
  and cheese gnocci, 59
  and cheese scones, 60
  salad filling for open sandwiches, 88
Prawns and shrimps
  curry mayonnaise and prawns filling
    for tartlets, 135
  kebabs, cold, 27
  mayonnaise fillings for tartlets, 135
  open sandwiches with prawns, 87
  paprika mayonnaise fillings for
    tartlets, 135
  pizzas, 162
  prawn and cream cheese dip, 74
  prawn and cream cheese pâté, 95
  prawn and hollandaise sauce filling for
    bouchées, 153
  prawn filling for bouchées, 152
  prawn filling for croustades, 111
  prawn filling for hot canapés, 109
  prawn filling for hot tartlets, 121
  prawn fritters, 62
  prawn in tomato sauce filling for
    tartlets, 130
  prawn mayonnaise filling for savoury
    éclairs, 160
  quiches, 127
  scrambled egg and prawns filling for
    hot canapés, 105
  scrambled egg and prawns filling for
    tartlets, 136
  scrambled egg and prawns (or
    shrimps and whitefish) filling for
    croustades, 111
  shrimps in butter, 80
  Spanish prawns and garlic filling for
    canapés, 109
  Spanish prawns and garlic filling for
    tartlets, 130
  Spanish prawns filling for pirogs, 144
Prunes, stuffed, in bacon rolls, 33
Puff pastry, 176
  apple and sausage rolls, 154
  bouchées, 151
  burek, 172
  cheese horseshoes, 156
  little pies, 154
  pinwheels, 156
  pirogs, 172
  salmon or tunafish puffs, 156
  sausage and salami rolls, 154

sausage rolls, 153
turnovers, 154

Quiches
  asparagus, 125
  gruyère, 126
  leek, 125
  Lorraine, 124
  à la Niçoise, 124
  onion with black olives, 126
  prawn, 127
  salami and cream cheese, 127
  spinach and ham, 125
  tuna and anchovy, 126

Reindeer, smoked
  filling for open sandwiches, 87
  pinwheels, 81
  tunnel rolls, 82
Roes
  devilled, filling for tartlets, 131
  soft roes on sticks, 38

Salami
  canapés, 78
  and cheese filling for tartlets, 122
  cheese, sausage and salami rolls, 147
  and cream cheese quiche, 127
  filling for open sandwiches, 87
  pizzas, 162
  puff pastry sausage and salami rolls,
    154
  sausage and salami rolls, 119
Salmon
  canapés, 80
  and cream cheese balls, 47
  and cucumber filling for tartlets, 133
  filling for bouchées, 152
  filling for savoury éclairs, 159
  mousse filling for tartlets, 137
  puffs, 156
  in savoury sauce filling for croustades,
    111
  and scrambled egg filling for
    croustades, 111
  and tunafish filling for pirogs, 141
Salmon, smoked
  dip, 72
  filling for hot canapés, 107
  filling for pinwheels, 81
  for open sandwiches, 87
  pâté, 94
  pâté filling for pinwheels, 81
Sambusak, 173
  cheese fillings, 173
  other fillings, 174
Sandwiches
  baby English, 82
  bacon and mushroom (hot), 114